C000216551

LONDON'S
GREAT
PLAGUE

LONDON'S GREAT PLAGUE

SAMUEL PEPYS

AMBERLEY

First published 2014

Amberley Publishing
The Hill, Stroud
Gloucestershire, GL5 4EP

www.amberley-books.com

Copyright © Amberley Publishing 2014

The right of Amberley Publishing to be identified as the Author
of this work has been asserted in accordance with the
Copyrights, Designs and Patents Act 1988.

All rights reserved. No part of this book may be reprinted
or reproduced or utilised in any form or by any electronic,
mechanical or other means, now known or hereafter invented,
including photocopying and recording, or in any information
storage or retrieval system, without the permission in writing
from the Publishers.

British Library Cataloguing in Publication Data.
A catalogue record for this book is available from the British Library.

ISBN 978 1 4456 3782 2 (paperback)
ISBN 978 1 4456 3794 5 (ebook)

Typeset in 10pt on 12pt Sabon.
Typesetting and Origination by Amberley Publishing.
Printed in the UK.

October 1663 (King Charles II)

19th. Waked with a very high wind, and said to my
wife, 'I pray God I hear not of the death of any great
person, this wind is so high!' fearing that the Queen
might be dead. So up; and going by coach with Sir W.
Batten and Sir J. Minnes to St James's, they tell me that
Sir W. Compton, who it is true had been a little sickly
for a week or fortnight, but was very well upon Friday
at night last at the Tangier Committee with us, was
dead, died yesterday: at which I was most exceedingly
surprised, he being, and so all the world saying that
he was one of the worthiest men and best officers of
State now in England; and so in my conscience he was:
of the best temper, valour, ability of mind, integrity,
worth, fine person, and diligence of any one man he
hath left behind him in the three kingdoms; and yet
not forty years old, or if so, that is all. I find the sober
men of the Court troubled for him; and yet not so as
to hinder or lessen their mirth, talking, laughing, and
eating, drinking, and doing everything else, just as if
there was no such thing.

Coming to St James's, I hear that the Queen did sleep five hours pretty well tonight, and that she waked and gargled her mouth, and to sleep again; but that her pulse beats fast, beating twenty to the King's or my Lady Suffolk's eleven; but not so strong as it was. It seems she was so ill as to be shaved, and pigeons put to her feet, and to have the extreme unction given her by the priests, who were so long about it that the doctors were angry. The King, they all say, is most fondly disconsolate for her, and weeps by her, which makes her weep; which one this day told me he reckons a good sign, for that it carries away some rheume from the head. This morning Captain Allen tells me how the famous Ned Mullins, by a slight fall, broke his leg at the ancle, which festered; and he had his leg cut off on Saturday, but so ill done, notwithstanding all the great chyrurgeons about the town at the doing of it, that they fear he will not live with it. Being invited to dinner to my Lord Barkeley's, and so, not knowing how to spend our time till noon, Sir W. Batten and I took coach and to the Coffee house in Cornhill; where much talk about the Turke's proceedings, and that the plague is got to Amsterdam, brought by a ship from Algiers; and it is also carried to Hambrough. The Duke says the King purposes to forbid any of their ships coming into the river. The Duke also told us of several Christian commanders (French) gone over to the Turkes to serve them; and upon enquiry, I find that the King of France does by this aspire to the Empire, and so to get the Crown of Spain also upon the death of the King, which is very probable, it seems. Back to St James's, and there dined with my Lord Barkeley and his lady, where Sir G. Carteret, Sir W. Batten, and myself, with two gentlemen more: my lady, and one of the ladies of honour to the Duchess – no handsome woman, but a most excellent hand. A fine French dinner. To dinner to my Lord Mayor's, being invited, where was the farmers of the Customes, my Lord Chancellor's three sons, and other great and much company, and a very great noble dinner, as this Mayor is good for nothing else. No extraordinary discourse of anything, every man being intent upon his dinner.

31st. To my great sorrow find myself 43*l* worse than I was the last month, which was then 760*l*, and now it is but 717*l*. But it hath chiefly arisen from my layings-out in clothes for myself and wife; viz., for her about 12*l*, and for myself 55*l*, or thereabouts; having made myself a velvet cloak, two new cloth shirts, black, plain both; a new shag gown, trimmed with gold buttons and twist, with a new hat, and silk tops for my legs, and many other things, being resolved henceforward to go like myself. And also two perriwiggs, one whereof cost me 3*l*, and the other 40*s*. I have worn neither yet, but will begin next week, God willing. I having laid out in clothes for myself, and wife, and for her closet and other things without, these two months this, and the last, besides household expenses of victualls, etc., above 110*l*. But I hope I shall with more comfort labour to get more, and with better success than when, for want of clothes, I was forced to sneak like a beggar. The Queen continues light-headed, but in hopes to recover. The plague is much in Amsterdam, and we in fear of it here, which God defend. The Turk goes on mighty in the Emperor's dominions, and the Princes cannot agree among themselves how to go against him.

November 1663

26th. The plague, it seems, grows more and more at Amsterdam; and we are going upon making of all ships coming from thence and Hambrough, or any other infected places, to perform their Quarantine, for thirty days, as Sir Richard Browne expressed it in the order of the Council, contrary to the import of the word, though, in the general acceptation, it signifies now the thing, not the time spent in doing it, in Holehaven; a thing never done by us before.

May 1664

4th. To my cozen Scott's. There condoled with him the loss of my cozen his wife, and talked about his matters, as attorney to my father, in his administering to my brother Tom. He tells me we are like to receive some shame about the business of his bastarde with Jack Noble; but no matter, so it cost us no money. The plague increases at Amsterdam.

June 1664

16th. I lay in my drawers, and stockings, and waistcoat till five of the clock, and so up; and, being well pleased with our frolick, walked to Knightsbridge, and there eat a mess of cream, and so to St James's, and I to Whitehall, and took coach, and found my wife well got home last night, and now in bed. The talk upon the 'Change is, that De Ruyter is dead, with fifty men of his own ship, of the plague, at Cales: that the Holland Embassador here do endeavour to sweeten us with fair words: and things like to be peaceable. With my cozen Richard Pepys upon the 'Change, about supplying us with bewpers from Norwich, which I should be glad of, if cheap.

22nd. To the 'Change and Coffee House, where great talk of the Dutch preparing of sixty sail of ships. The plague grows mightily among them, both at sea and land.

✶ DICT

August 1664

25th. Met with a printed copy of the King's commission for the repair of Paul's, which is very large, and large power for collecting money, and recovering of all people that had bought or sold formerly anything belonging to the church. And here I find my Lord Mayor of the city set in order before the Archbishop or any nobleman, though all the greatest officers of the state are there. But yet I do not hear, by my Lord Barkely, who is one of them, that anything is like to come of it. No news, only the plague is very hot still, and encreases among the Dutch.

September 1664

24th. Comes one Phillips, who is concerned in the Lottery, and from whom I collected much concerning that business. He told me that Monsieur du Puy, that is so great a man at the Duke of York's, and this man's great opponent, is a knave, and by quality but a tailor. We were told today of a Dutch ship of 300 or 400 tons, where all the men were dead of the plague, and the ship cast ashore at Gottenburgh.

April 1665

30th. (Lord's day.) I with great joy find myself to have gained, this month, above 100*l* clear, and in the whole to be worth 1,400*l*. Thus I end this month in great content as to my estate and gettings: in much trouble as to the pains I have taken, and the rubs I expect to meet with, about the business of Tangier. The fleet, with about 106 ships upon the coast of Holland, in sight of the Dutch, within the Texel. Great fears of the sickness here in the City, it being said that two or three houses are already shut up. God preserve us all!

May 1665

24th. To the Coffee house, where all the news is of the Dutch being gone out, and of the plague growing upon us in this town; and of remedies against it: some saying one thing, and some another.

June 1665

10th. In the evening home to supper; and there, to my great trouble, hear that the plague is come into the City, though it hath, these three or four weeks since its beginning, been wholly out of the City; but where should it begin but in my good friend and neighbour's, Dr Burnett, in Fenchurch Street; which, in both points, troubles me mightily.

11th. (Lord's day.) Up, and expected long a new suit; but, coming not, dressed myself in my new black silk camelott suit; and, when fully ready, comes my new one of coloured Ferrandin, which my wife puts me out of love with, which vexes me. At noon, by invitation, comes my two cozen Joyces and their wives – my aunt James and he-cozen Harman – his wife being ill. Had a good dinner for them, and as merry as I could be in such company. They being gone, I out of doors a little, to show, forsooth, my new suit. I saw poor Dr Burnett's door shut; but he hath, I hear, gained great good-will among his neighbours: for he discovered it himself first,

✳ DICT

and caused himself to be shut up of his own accord; which was very handsome.

15th. Up, and put on my new stuff suit with close knees, which becomes me most nobly, as my wife says. At noon, put on my first laced band, all lace; and to Kate Joyce's to dinner, where my mother, wife, and abundance of their friends, and good usage. At Woolwich, discoursed with Mr Sheldon about my bringing my wife down for a month or two to his house, which he approves of, and, I think, will be very convenient. This day, the News-book, upon Mr Moore's showing L'Estrange, Captain Ferrer's letter, did do my Lord Sandwich great right as to the late victory. The Duke of York not yet come to town. The town grows very sickly, and people to be afraid of it: there dying this last week of the plague 112, from forty-three the week before: whereof but one in Fenchurch Streete, and one in Broad Streete, by the Treasurer's office.

17th. At the office find Sir W. Pen come home, who looks very well; and I am gladder to see him than otherwise I should be, because of my hearing so well of him for his serviceableness in this late great action. It struck me very deep this afternoon going with a hackney coach from Lord Treasurer's down Holborne, the coachman I found to drive easily and easily, at last stood still, and come down hardly able to stand, and told me that he was suddenly struck very sick, and almost blind he could not see; so I 'light, and went into another coach, with a sad heart for the poor man and for myself also, lest he should have been struck with the plague. Sir

John Lawson, I hear, is worse than yesterday: the King went to see him today most kindly. It seems his wound is not very bad; but he hath a fever, a thrush,* and a hiccough, all three together, which are, it seems, very bad symptoms.

20th. Thanks-giving-day for victory over the Dutch. To the Dolphin Taverne, where all we officers of the Navy met with the Commissioners of the Ordnance by agreement, and dined: where good music at my direction. Our club come to 34s a man, nine of us. By water to Fox Hall,* and there walked an hour alone, observing the several humours of the citizens that were there this holiday, pulling off cherries, and God knows what. This day I informed myself that there died four or five at Westminster of the Plague, in several houses, upon Sunday last, in Bell Alley, over against the Palace-gate; yet people do think that the number will be fewer in the town than it was the last week. The Dutch are come out again with twenty sail under Bankert: supposed gone to the Northward, to meet their East India fleet.

21st. I find our talleys will not be money in less than sixteen months, which is a sad thing for the King to pay all that interest for every penny he spends; and, which is strange, the goldsmiths with whom I spoke do declare that they will not be moved to part with money upon the increase of their consideration of ten per cent, which they have. I find all the town almost going out of town, the coaches and waggons being all full of people going into the country.

* DICT (could this be an English translation for "VAUXHALL" (Fr.) ?

22nd. In great pain whether to send my mother into the country today or no; I hearing, by my people, that the poor wretch hath a mind to stay a little longer, and I cannot blame her. At last, I resolved to put it to her, and she agreed to go because of the sickness in town, and my intentions of removing my wife. She was to the last unwilling to go, but would not say so, but put it off till she lost her place in the coach, and was fain to ride in the waggon part.

Sends both his wife & mother to the country".

23rd. To a Committee for Tangier, where, unknown to me, comes my Lord Sandwich, who, it seems, come to town last night. After the Committee was up, my Lord Sandwich did take me aside in the robe-chamber, telling me how much the Duke and Mr Coventry did, both in the fleet and here, make of him, and that in some opposition to the Prince; and, as a more private passage, he told me that he hath been with them both when they have made sport of the Prince, and laughed at him: yet that all the discourse of the town, and the printed relation, should not give him one word of honour, my Lord thinks very strange; he assuring me, that, though by accident the Prince was in the van in the beginning of the fight for the first pass, yet, all the rest of the day, my Lord was in the van, and continued so. That, notwithstanding all this noise of the Prince, he had hardly a shot in his side, nor a man killed, whereas he [Lord Sandwich] above thirty in her hull, and not one mast whole nor yard; but the most battered ship of the fleet, and lost most men, saving Captain Smith of the *Mary*. That the most the Duke did was almost out of gun-shot; but that, indeed, the Duke did come up to my Lord's rescue, after he had a great while fought with four of them. How poorly Sir John Lawson performed, notwithstanding all that was said of him; and how his ship turned out of the way, while Sir J. Lawson himself was upon the deck, to the endangering of the whole fleet. It therefore troubles my Lord, that Mr Coventry should not mention a word of him in his relation. I did, in answer, offer that I was sure the relation was not compiled by Mr Coventry, but by L'Estrange, out of several letters, as I could witness, and that Mr Coventry's letter that he did give the Duke of Albemarle he as much writ as the Prince; for I myself read it first, and then copied it out, which I promised to show my Lord, with which he was something satisfied. From that discourse my Lord did begin to tell me how much he was concerned to dispose of his children, and would have my advice and help; and propounded to match my Lady Jemimah to Sir G. Carteret's eldest son, which I approved of, and did undertake the speaking with him about it as from myself, which my Lord liked. To one Mr Finch, one of the Commissioners of the Excise, to be informed about some things of the Excise, in order to our settling matters therein better. I find him a very discreet, grave person. Creed and I took boat, and to Fox Hall, where we spent two or three hours talking of several matters very soberly and contentfully to me, which, with the ayre and pleasure of the garden, was a great refreshment to me, and methinks that which we ought to joy ourselves in. Home, by hackney-coach, which is become a very dangerous passage now-a-days, the sickness increasing mightily.

26th. To the Committee of Tangier, where my Lord Treasurer was, the first and only time he ever was

* See p 19 Above
† see p 18 Above

there, and did promise us 15,000*l* for Tangier, and no more, which will be short. With Creed to the King's Head ordinary, and good sport with one Mr Nicholls, a prating coxcombe, that would be thought a poet, but would not be got to repeat any of his verses. Home, and there find my wife's brother, and his wife, a pretty little modest woman, where they come to dine with my wife. He did come to desire my assistance for a living, and, upon his good promises of care, and that it should be no burden to me, I did say and promise I would think of finding something for him, and the rather because his wife seems a pretty discreet young thing, and humble, and he, above all things, desirous to do something to maintain her, telling me sad stories of what she endured in Holland; and I hope it will not be burdensome. The plague encreases mightily, I this day seeing a house, at a bitt-maker's, over against St Clement's church, in the open street, shut up, which is a sad sight.

In the coach, class of transport

29th. By water to White Hall, where the Court full of waggons and people ready to go out of town. This end of the town every day grows very bad of the plague. The Mortality Bill is come to 267; which is about ninety more than the last: and of these but four in the City, which is a great blessing to us. Took leave again of Mr Coventry; though I hope the Duke is not gone to stay, and so do others too. Home; calling at Somerset House, where all were packing up too: the Queen-Mother setting out for France this day, to drink Bourbon waters this year, she being in a consumption; and intends not to come till winter come twelve-months.

* *A serious disease: see* Dict

30th. To White Hall,* to the Duke of Albemarle, who I find at Secretary Bennet's, there being now no other great statesman, I think, but my Lord Chancellor, in town. At night, back by water, and in the dark and against the tide, shot the bridge, groping with their pole for the way, which troubled me before I got through. So home, about one or two o'clock in the morning, my family at a great loss what was become of me. Thus this book of two years ends. Myself and family in good health, consisting of myself and wife, Mercer, her woman, Mary, Alice and Susan, our maids, and Tom, my boy. In a sickly time of the plague growing on. Having upon my hands the troublesome care of the Treasury of Tangier, with great sums drawn upon me, and nothing to pay them with: also the business of the office great. Considering of removing my wife to Woolwich; she lately busy in learning to paint, with great pleasure and successe. All other things well; especially a new interest I am making, by a match in hand between the eldest son of Sir G. Carteret, and my Lady Jemimah Montagu. The Duke of York gone down to the fleet; but all suppose not with intent to stay there, as it is not fit, all men conceive, he should.

* Now a street name

July 1665 *The Plague goes grimly on*

1st. To the Duke of Albemarle's, by appointment, to give him an account of some disorder in the Yard at Portsmouth, by workmen going away of their own accord, for lack of money to get work of haymaking, or anything else, to earn themselves bread. To Westminster, where, I hear, the sickness increases greatly. Sad at the news, that seven or eight houses in Burying Hall Street are shut up of the plague.

3rd. The season growing so sickly, that it is much to be feared how a man can escape having a share with others in it, for which the good Lord God bless me! or make me fitted to receive it.

5th. Advised about sending my wife's bedding and things today to Woolwich, in order to her removal thither. Mr Coventry tells me how matters are ordered in the fleet: my Lord Sandwich goes Admiral; under him Sir G. Ascue, and Sir T. Teddiman: Vice-Admiral, Sir W. Pen; and under him Sir W. Barkeley, and Sir Jos.

Jordan: Rear-Admiral Sir Thomas Allen; and under him Sir Christopher Mings, and Captain Harman. Walked round to White Hall, the Park being quite locked up; and I observed a house shut up this day in the Pell Mell, where, heretofore, in Cromwell's time, we young men used to keep our weekly clubs. Sir G. Carteret do now take all my Lord Sandwich's business to heart, and makes it the same with his own. He tells me how at Chatham it was proposed to my Lord Sandwich to be joined with the Prince in the command of the fleet, which he was most willing to; but, when it come to the Prince, he was quite against it; saying, there could be no government, but that it would be better to have two fleets, and neither under the command of the other, which he would not agree to. So the King was not pleased; but, ~~without~~ any unkindness, did order the fleet to be ordered as above, as to the Admirals and commands: so the Prince is come up; and Sir G. Carteret, I remember, had this word thence, that, says he, by this means, though the King told him that it would be but for this expedition, yet I believe we shall keep him out for altogether. He tells me how my Lord was much troubled at Sir W. Pen's being ordered forth, as it seems he is to go to Solebay, and with the best fleet he can, to go forth, and no notice taken of my Lord Sandwich going after him, and having the command over him. By water to Woolwich, where I found my wife come, and her two maids, and very prettily accommodated they will be; and I left them going to supper, grieved in my heart to part with my wife, being worse by much without her, though some trouble there is in having the care of a family at home this plague time.

* two independant Fleets

6th. Alderman Backewell is ordered abroad upon some private score with a great sum of money; wherein I was instrumental the other day in shipping him away. It seems some of his creditors have taken notice of it, and he was like to be broke yesterday in his absence: Sir G. Carteret tells me that the King and the kingdom must as good as fall with that man at this time; and that he was forced to get 4,000*l* himself to answer Backewell's people's occasions, or he must have broke; but committed this to me as a great secret. I could not see Lord Brouncker, nor had much mind, one of the two great houses within two doors of him being shut up: and, Lord! the number of houses visited, which this day I observed through the town, quite round in my way, by Long Lane and London Wall. To Sir W. Batten, and spent the evening at supper; and, among other discourse, the rashness of Sir John Lawson, for breeding up his daughter so high and proud, refusing a man of great interest, Sir W. Barkeley, to match her with a melancholy fellow, Colonel Norton's son, of no interest nor good nature nor generosity at all, giving her 6,000*l*, when the other would have taken her with two when he himself knew that he was not worth the money himself in all the world, he did give her that portion, and is since dead, and left his wife and two daughters beggars, and the other gone away with 6,000*l*, and no content in it, through the ill qualities of her father-in-law and husband, who, it seems, though a pretty woman, contracted for her as if he had been buying a horse; and, worst of all, is now of no use to serve the mother and two little sisters in any stead at Court, whereas, the other might have done what he would for her: so here is an end of this family's pride, which, with good care, might have been what they would, and done well. Sir W. Pen, it seems, sailed last night from Solebay, with about sixty sail of ships, and my Lord Sandwich in the Prince and some others, it seems, going after them to overtake them.

9th. (Lord's day.) To Sir G. Carteret, and there find my Lady in her chamber, not very well, but looks the worst almost that ever I did see her in my life. It seems her drinking of the water at Tunbridge did almost kill her. Received with most extraordinary kindness by my Lady Carteret and her children, and dined most nobly. I took occasion to have much discourse with Mr Ph. Carteret, and find him a very modest man; and I think verily of mighty good nature, and pretty understanding. He did give me a good account of the fight with the Dutch. Took boat and home, and there shifted myself into my black silk suit; and, having promised Harman yesterday, I to his house, which I find very mean, and mean company. His wife very ill: I could not see her. Here I, with her father and Kate Joyce, who was also very ill, were godfathers and godmothers to his boy, and was christened Will. Mr Meriton christened him. The most observable thing I found there to my content, was to hear him and his clerk tell me, that in this parish of Michell's Cornhill, one of the middlemost parishes, and a great one of the town, there hath, notwithstanding this sickliness, been buried of any disease, man, woman, or child, not one for thirteen months last past; which is very strange. And the like, in a good degree, in most other parishes, I hear, saving only of the plague in them. Down to my Lady Carteret's. It is mighty pretty to think how my poor Lady Sandwich, between her and me, is doubtfull whether her daughter will like of the match or no, and how troubled she is for fear of it, which I do not fear at all, and desire her not to do it, but her fear is the most discreet and pretty that ever I did see.

10th. Having a coach of Mr Povy's attending me, by appointment, in order to my coming to dine at his country-house, at Branford, where he and his family is, I went, and Mr Tasbrough with me therein, it being a pretty chariot, but most inconvenient as to the horses throwing dust and dirt into one's eyes, and upon one's clothes. Creed rode before, and Mr Povy and I after him in the chariot; and I was set down by him at the Parke pale, where one of his saddle-horses was ready for me, he himself not daring to come into the house or be seen, because that a servant of his, out of his house, happened to be sick, but is not yet dead, but was never suffered to come into his house after he was ill. But this opportunity was taken to injure Povy, and most horribly he is abused by some persons hereupon, and his fortune, I believe, quite broke; but that he hath a good heart to bear, or a cunning one to conceal his evil. It is, I perceive, an unpleasing thing to be at Court, everybody being fearful one of another, and all so sad enquiring after the plague, so that I stole away by my horse to Kingston, and there, with much trouble, was forced to press two sturdy rogues to carry me to London, and met at the water-side with Mr Charnocke, Sir Philip Warwick's clerk, who had been with company, and was quite foxed. I took him with me in my boat, and so away to Richmond, and there, by night, walked with him to Mortlake, a very pretty walk, and there staid a good while.

12th. After doing what business I could in the morning, it being a solemn fast-day for the plague growing upon us, I took boat, and down to Deptford, where I stood with great pleasure an hour or two by my Lady Sandwich's bedside, talking to her, she lying prettily in bed, of my Lady Jemimah's being from my Lady Pickering's when our letters come to that place; she being at my Lord Montagu's, at Boughton. The truth is, I had received letters of it two days ago, but had dropped them, and was in a very extraordinary strait what to do for them, or what account to give my Lady: but sent to Mortlake, where I had been the night before, and there they were found, which with mighty joy come safe to me; but all ending with satisfaction to my Lady and me, though I find my Lady Carteret not much pleased with this delay, and principally because of the plague, which renders it unsafe to stay long at Deptford. I eat a bit, my Lady Carteret being the most kind lady in the world, and so took boat, and a fresh boat at the Tower, and so up the river, against tide all the way, I having lost it by staying prating to and with my Lady; and, from before one, made it seven before we got to Hampton-Court; and, when I come there, all business was over, saving my finding Mr Coventry at his chamber; and so away to my boat, and all night upon the water, and come home by two o'clock, shooting the bridge at that time of night. Heard Mr Williamson repeat at Hampton-Court, today, how the King of France hath lately set out a most high arrest against the Pope, which is reckoned very lofty and high.

13th. By water, at night late, to Sir G. Carteret's, but, there being no oars to carry me, I was fain to call a skuller that had a gentleman already in it, and he proved a man of love to music, and he and I sung together the way down with great pleasure. Above 700 died of the plague this week.

17th. Up all of us, and to billiards; my Lady Wright, Mr Carteret, myself, and everybody. By and by, the young couple left together. Anon to dinner; and after dinner Mr Carteret took my advice about giving to the servants 10*l* among them, which he did, by leaving it to the chief man-servant, Mr Medows, to do for him. Before we went, I took my Lady Jem. apart, and would know how she liked this gentleman, and whether she was under any difficulty concerning him. She blushed, and hid her face awhile; but at last I forced her to tell me. She answered, that she could readily obey what her father and mother had done; which was all she could say, or I expect. But, Lord! to see among other things, how all these great people here are afraid of London, being doubtful of anything that comes from thence, or that hath lately been there, that I was forced to say that I lived wholly at Woolwich. So anon took leave, and for London. In our way, Mr Carteret did give me mighty thanks for my care and pains for him, and is mightily pleased, though the truth is, my Lady Jem. hath carried herself with mighty discretion and gravity, not being forward at all in any degree, but mighty serious in her answers to him, as by what he says and I observed, I collect. To Deptford, where mighty welcome, and brought the good news of all being pleased. Mighty mirth of my giving them an account of all; but the young man could not be got to say one word before me or my Lady Sandwich of his adventures; but, by what he afterwards related to his father and mother and sisters, he gives an account that pleases them mightily. Here Sir G. Carteret would have me lie all night, which I did most nobly, better than ever I did in my life; Sir G. Carteret being mighty kind to me, leading me to my chamber; and all their care now is, to have the business ended; and they have reason, because the sickness puts all out of order, and they cannot safely stay where they are.

18th. To the 'Change, where a little business, and a very thin Exchange; and so walked through London to the Temple, where I took water for Westminster to the Duke of Albemarle, to wait on him, and so to Westminster Hall, and there paid for my news-books, and did give Mrs Michell, who is going out of town because of the sickness, and her husband, a pint of wine. I was much troubled this day to hear, at Westminster, how the officers do bury the dead in the open Tuttle-fields, pretending want of room elsewhere; whereas, the New Chapel church-yard was walled in at the public charge in the last plague-time, merely for want of room; and now none, but such as are able to pay dear for it, can be buried there.

20th. To Deptford, and after dinner saw my Lady Sandwich and Mr Carteret and his two sisters over the water, going to Dagenhams, and my Lady Carteret toward Cranburne. Walked to Redriffe, where I hear the sickness is, and indeed is scattered almost every where, there dying 1,089 of the plague this week. My Lady Carteret did this day give me a bottle of plague-water home with me. I received yesterday a letter from my Lord Sandwich, giving me thanks for my care about their marriage business, and desiring it to be dispatched, that no disappointment may happen therein. Lord! to see how the plague spreads! It being now all over King's Street, at the Axe, and next door to it, and in other places.

21st. To Anthony Joyce's, and there broke to him my desire to have Pall married to Harman, whose wife, poor woman, is lately dead, to my trouble, I loving her very much, and he will consider it. Late in my chamber, setting some papers in order; the plague growing very raging, and my apprehensions of it great.

22nd. The Duke of Albemarle being gone to dinner to my Lord of Canterbury's, I thither, and there walked and viewed the new hall, a new old-fashioned hall, as much as possible begun, and means left for the ending of it, by Bishop Juxon. To Fox Hall, where to the Spring garden; but I do not see one guest there, the town being so empty of anybody to come thither. Only, while I was there, a poor woman come to scold with the master of the house that a kinswoman, I think, of her's, that was nearly dead of the plague, might be buried in the church-yard; for, for her part, she should not be buried in the commons, as they said she should. I by coach home, not meeting with but two coaches and but two carts from White Hall to my own house, that I could observe, and the streets mighty thin of people. I met this

noon with Dr Burnett, who told me, and I find in the
news book this week that he posted upon the 'Change,
that whoever did spread the report that, instead of
dying of the plague, his servant was by him killed, it
was forgery, and shewed me the acknowledgment of
the Master of the pest-house, and that his servant died
of a bubo on his right groin, and two spots on his right
thigh, which is the plague. All the news is great: that we
must of necessity fall out with France, for He will side
with the Dutch against us. That Alderman Backewell
is gone over, which indeed he is, with money, and that
Ostend is in our present possession. But it is strange to
see how poor Alderman Backewell is like to be put to it
in his absence, Mr Shaw, his right hand, being ill. And
the Alderman's absence gives doubts to people, and
I perceive they are in great straits for money, besides
what Sir G. Carteret told me about fourteen days ago.
Our fleet, under my Lord Sandwich, being about the
latitude 55½, which is a great secret, to the northward
of the Texel.

25th. Our good humour in everybody continuing, I slept
till seven o'clock. Sad the story of the plague in the City,
it growing mightily. This day my Lord Brouncker did
give me Grant's book upon the Bills of Mortality, new
printed and enlarged. To my office: thence by coach to
the Duke of Albemarle's, not meeting one coach, going
nor coming. This day come a letter to me from Paris,
from my Lord Hinchingbroke, about his coming over;
and I have sent this night an order from the Duke of
Albemarle for a ship of thirty-six guns to go to Calais
to fetch him.

26th. To Greenwich, to the Park, where I heard the King and Duke are come by water this morn from Hampton Court. They asked me several questions. The King mightily pleased with his new buildings there. I followed them to Castle's ship, in building, and there met Sir W. Batten, and thence to Sir G. Carteret's, where all the morning with them; they not having any but the Duke of Monmouth, and Sir W. Killigrew, and one gentleman, and a page more. Great variety of talk, and was often led to speak to the King and Duke. By and by they to dinner, and all to dinner and sat down to the King, saving myself, which, though I could not in modesty expect, yet, God forgive my pride! I was sorry I was there, that Sir W. Batten should say that he could sit down where I could not. The King having dined, he came down, and I went in the barge with him, I sitting at the door. Down to Woolwich, and there I just saw and kissed my wife, and saw some of her painting, which is very curious; and away again to the King, and back again with him in the barge, hearing him and the Duke talk, and seeing and observing their manner of discourse. And, God forgive me! though I admire them with all the duty possible, yet the more a man considers and observes them, the less he finds of difference between them and other men, though, blessed be God! they are both princes of great nobleness and spirits. The Duke of Monmouth is the most skittish leaping gallant that ever I saw, always in action, vaulting or leaping, or clambering. Sad news of the death of so many in the parish of the plague, forty last night. The bell always going. To the Exchange, where I went up and sat talking with my beauty, Mrs Batelier, a great while, who is indeed one of the finest women I ever saw in my life. This day poor Robin Shaw at Backewell's died, and Backewell himself now in Flanders. The King himself asked about Shaw, and being told he was dead, said he was very sorry for it. The sickness has got into our parish this week, and is got, indeed, every where; so that I begin to think of setting things in order, which I pray God enable me to put, both as to soul and body.

28th. Set out with my Lady Sandwich all alone with her with six horses to Dagenhams; going by water to the Ferry. And a pleasant going, and a good discourse; and, when there, very merry, and the young couple now well acquainted. But, Lord! to see in what fear all the people here do live. How they are afraid of us that come to them, insomuch that I am troubled at it, and wish myself away. But some cause they have; for the chaplain, with whom, but a week or two ago, we were here mighty high disputing, is since fallen into a fever, and dead, being gone hence to a friend's a good way off. A sober and a healthful man. These considerations make us all hasten the marriage, and resolve it upon Monday next, which is three days before we intended it.

29th. Up betimes, and, after viewing some of my wife's pictures, which now she is come to do very finely, to the office. At noon to dinner, where I hear that my Will is come in thither, and laid down upon my bed, ill of the headache, which put me into extraordinary fear; and I studied all I could to get him out of the house, and set my people to work to do it without discouraging him, and myself went forth to the Old Exchange to pay my fair Batelier for some linnen, and took leave of her, they breaking up shop for a while; and so by coach to Kate Joyce's, and there used all the vehemence and rhetorique I could to get her husband to let her go down to Brampton, but I could not prevail with him; he urging some simple reasons, but most that of profit, minding the house, and the distance, if either of them should be ill. However, I did my best, and more than I had a mind to do, but that I saw him so resolved against it, while she was mightily troubled at it. At last he yielded she should go to Windsor, to some friends there; so I took my leave of them, believing it is great odds that we ever all see one another again; for I dare not go any more to that end of the town. Will is gone to his lodging, and is likely to do well, it being only the headache.

30th. (Lord's day.) Up, and in my night-gown, cap, and neckcloth, undressed, all day long lost not a minute, but in my chamber, setting my Tangier accounts to rights. Will is very well again. It was a sad noise to hear our bell to toll and ring so often today, either for deaths or burials; I think, five or six times.

31st. Up, and very betimes by six o'clock at Deptford, and there find Sir G. Carteret, and my Lady ready to go: I being in my new-coloured silk suit, and coat trimmed with gold buttons and gold broad lace round my hands, very rich and fine. By water to the Ferry, where, when we come, no coach there; and tide of ebb so far spent as the horse-boat could not get off on the other side of the river to bring away the coach. So we were fain to stay there in the unlucky Isle of Dogs, in a chill place, the morning cool, and wind fresh, above two if not three hours, to our great discontent. Yet, being upon a pleasant errand, and seeing that it could not be helped, we did bear it very patiently; and it was worth my observing to see how, upon these two scores, Sir G. Carteret, the most passionate man in the world, and that was in greatest haste to be gone, did bear with it, and very pleasant all the while, at least, not troubled so much as to fret and storm at it. Anon the coach comes: in the mean time, there coming a News thither with his horse to go over, and told us he did come from Islington this morning; and that Proctor, the vintner, of the Mitre, in Wood Street, and his son, are dead this morning there, of the plague: he having laid out abundance of money there, and was the greatest vintner for some time in London for great entertainments. We, fearing the canonical hour would be past before we got thither, did, with a great deal of unwillingness, send away the licence and wedding-ring. So that when we come, though we drove hard with six horses, yet we found them gone from home; and, going towards the church, met them coming from church, which troubled us. But, however, that trouble was soon over; hearing it was well done: they being both in their old clothes: my Lord Crewe giving her, there being three coachfulls of them. The young lady, mighty sad, which troubled me; but yet I think it was only her gravity in a little greater degree than usual. All saluted her, but I did not, till my Lady Sandwich did ask me whether I saluted her or no. So to dinner, and very merry we were; but in such a sober way as never almost any thing was in so great families: but it was much better. After dinner, company divided, some to

cards, others to talk. My Lady Sandwich and I up to
settle accounts, and pay her some money. And mighty
kind she is to me, and would fain have had me gone
down for company with her to Hinchingbroke; but for
my life I cannot. At night to supper, and so to talk; and
which, methought, was the most extraordinary thing,
all of us to prayers as usual, and the young bride and
bridegroom too: and so, after prayers, soberly to bed;
only I got into the bridegroom's chamber while he
undressed himself, and there was very merry, till he
was called to the bride's chamber, and into bed they
went. I kissed the bride in bed, and so the curtains
drawn with the greatest gravity that could be, and
so good night. But the modesty and gravity of this
business was so decent, that it was to me indeed ten
times more delightful than if it had been twenty times
more merry and jovial. Whereas, I feared we must have
sat up all night, we did here all get good beds, and I lay
in the same I did before, with Mr Brisband, who is a
good scholar and sober man; and we lay in bed, getting
him to give me an account of Rome, which is the most
delightful talk a man can have of any traveller: and so
to sleep. Thus, I ended this month with the greatest joy
that ever I did any in my life, because I have spent the
greatest part of it with abundance of joy, and honour,
and pleasant journeys, and brave entertainments, and
without cost of money; and at last live to see the
business ended with great content on all sides. This
evening with Mr Brisband, speaking of enchantments
and spells, I telling him some of my charms; he told me
this, of his own knowledge, at Bourdeaux, in France.
The words were these:

Voyci un Corps mort,
Royde come un Baston,
Froid comme Marbre,
Leger come un Esprit,
Levons le au nom de Jesus Christ.

He saw four little girls, very young ones all kneeling
each of them upon one knee; and one begun the first
line, whispering in the ear of the next, and the second
to the third, and the third to the fourth, and she to the
first. Then the first begun the second line, and so round
quite through; and, putting each one finger only to a
boy that lay flat upon his back upon the ground, as if
he was dead; at the end of the words, they did with
their four fingers raise this boy as high as they could
reach; and Mr Brisband, being there, and wondering
at it, as also being afraid to see it, for they would have
had him to have bore a part in saying the words, in the
room of one of the little girls that was so young that
they could hardly make her learn to repeat the words,
did, for fear there might be some slight used in it by
the boy, or that the boy might be light, call the cook
of the house, a very lusty fellow, as Sir G. Carteret's
cook, who is very big: and they did raise him just in
the same manner. This is one of the strangest things I
ever heard, but he tells it me of his own knowledge,
and I do heartily believe it to be true. I enquired of
him whether they were Protestant or Catholic girls;
and he told me they were Protestant, which made it the
more strange to me. Thus we end this month, as I said,
after the greatest glut of content that ever I had; only
under some difficulty because of the plague, which
grows mightily upon us, the last week being about

1,700 or 1,800 of the plague. My Lord Sandwich at sea with a fleet of about 100 sail, to the Northward, expecting De Ruyter, or the Dutch East India fleet. My Lord Hinchingbroke coming over from France, and will meet his sister at Scott's-hall. Myself having obliged both these families in this business very much; as both my Lady and Sir G. Carteret and his Lady do confess exceedingly, and the latter do also now call me cozen, which I am glad of. So God preserve us all friends long, and continue health among us!

August 1665

2nd. Up, it being a public fast, as being the first Wednesday of the month, for the plague; within doors all day, and upon my monthly accounts late. I did find myself really worth 1,900*l*, for which the great God of Heaven and Earth be praised!

3rd. Up, and betimes to Deptford to Sir G. Carteret's, where, not knowing the horse which had been hired by Mr Unthwayt for me, I did desire Sir G. Carteret to let me ride his new 40*l* horse; and so to the ferry, where I was forced to stay a great while before I could get my horse brought over, and then mounted, and rode very finely to Dagenhams; all the way, people, citizens, walking to and fro, enquire how the plague is in the City this week by the Bill; which, by chance, at Greenwich, I had heard was 2,020 of the plague, and 3,000 and odd, of all diseases; but methought it was a sad question to be so often asked me. Coming to Dagenhams, I there met our company coming out of the house, having stayed as long as they could for

me; so I let them go a little way before, and went and
took leave of my Lady Sandwich, good woman, who
seems very sensible of my service, in this late business,
and having her directions in some things – among
others to get Sir G. Carteret and my Lord to settle
the portion, and what Sir G. Carteret is to settle, into
land, soon as may be, she not liking it should lie long
undone, for fear of death on either side. So took leave
of her, and down to the buttery, and eat a piece of
cold venison pie, and drank, and took some bread and
cheese in my hand; and so mounted after them, Mr
Marr very kindly staying to lead me the way. By and
by met my Lord Crewe returning; Mr Marr telling me,
by the way, how a maid servant of Mr John Wright's,
who lives thereabouts, falling sick of the plague, she
was removed to an out-house, and a nurse appointed
to look to her; who, being once absent, the maid got
out of the house at the window, and run away. The
nurse coming and knocking, and, having no answer,
believed she was dead, and went and told Mr Wright
so; who and his lady were in a great straight what
to do to get her buried. At last, resolved to go to
Burntwood, hard by, being in the parish, and there
get people to do it. But they would not: so he went
home full of trouble, and in the way met the wench
walking over the common, which frighted him worse
than before; and was forced to send people to take her,
which he did; and they got one of the pest-coaches,
and put her into it, to carry her to a pest-house. And,
passing in a narrow lane, Sir Anthony Browne, with
his brother and some friends in the coach, met this
coach with the curtains drawn close. The brother,
being a young man, and believing there might be some

lady in it that would not be seen, and the way being
narrow, he thrust his head out of his own into her
coach, and to look, and there saw somebody looking
very ill, and in a silk dress, and stunk mightily; which
the coachman also cried out upon. And presently they
come up to some people that stood looking after
it, and told our gallants that it was a maid of Mr
Wright's carried away sick of the plague; which put
the young gentleman into a fright had almost cost
him his life, but is now well again. I, overtaking our
young people, alight, and into the coach with them,
where mighty merry all the way; and anon come to
the Blockehouse, over against Gravesend, where we
staid a great while, in a little drinking-house. Sent
back our coaches to Dagenhams. I, by and by, by
boat to Gravesend, where no news of Sir G. Carteret
come yet: so back again, and fetched them all over,
but the two saddle-horses that were to go with us,
which could not be brought over in the horse-boat,
the wind and tide being against us, without towing;
so we had some difference with some watermen, who
would not tow them over under 20*s*, whereupon I
swore to send one of them to sea, and will do it. Anon
some others did it for 10*s*. By and by comes Sir G.
Carteret, and so we set out for Chatham: in my way
overtaking some company, wherein was a lady, very
pretty, riding singly, her husband in company with her.
We fell into talk, and I read a copy of verses, which her
husband showed me, and he discommended; but the
lady, commended: and I read them, so as to make the
husband turn and commend them. By and by he and
I fell into acquaintance, having known me formerly at
the Exchequer. His name is Nokes, over-against Bow

church. He was servant to Alderman Dashwood. We promised to meet, if ever we come both to London again; and, at parting, I had a fair salute on horseback, in Rochester streets, of the lady. My Lady Carteret come to Chatham in a coach, by herself, before us. Great mind they have to buy a little hacquenee that I rode on from Greenwich, for a woman's horse.

8th. To my office a little, and then to the Duke of Albemarle's about some business. The streets empty all the way, now, even in London, which is a sad sight. And to Westminster Hall, where talking, hearing very sad stories from Mrs Mumford; among others, of Mr Mitchell's son's family. And poor Will, that used to sell us ale at the Hall-door, his wife and three children died, all, I think, in a day. So home, through the City again, wishing I may have taken no ill in going; but I will go, I think, no more thither. The news of De Ruyter's coming home is certain; and told to the great disadvantage of our fleet, and the praise of De Ruyter; but it cannot be helped.

10th. My she-cozen Porter, the turner's wife, to tell me that her husband was carried to the Tower, for buying of some of the King's powder, and would have my help, but I could give her none, not daring to appear in the business. By and by to the office, where we sat all the morning; in great trouble to see the Bill this week rise so high, to above 4,000 in all, and of them above 3,000 of the plague. Home, to draw over anew my will, which I had bound myself by oath to dispatch by tomorrow night; the town growing so unhealthy, that a man cannot depend upon living two days.

11th. To the Exchequer, about striking new tallies, and I find the Exchequer, by proclamation, removing to Nonsuch. Setting my house, and all things, in the best order I can, lest it should please God to take me away, or force me to leave my house.

12th. Sent for by Sir G. Carteret, to meet him and my Lord Hinchingbroke at Deptford, but my Lord did not come thither, he having crossed the river at Gravesend to Dagenhams, whither I dare not follow him, they being afraid of me; but Sir G. Carteret says, he is a most sweet youth in every circumstance. Sir G. Carteret being in haste of going to the Duke of Albemarle and the Archbishop, he was pettish. The people die so, that now it seems they are fain to carry the dead to be buried by daylight, the nights not sufficing to do it in. And my Lord Mayor commands people to be within at nine at night all, as they say, that the sick may have liberty to go abroad for ayre. There is one also dead out of one of our ships at Deptford, which troubles us mightily – the *Providence*, fire-ship, which was just fitted to go to sea; but they tell me, today, no more sick on board. And this day W. Bodham tells me that one is dead at Woolwich, not far from the Ropeyard. I am told too, that a wife of one of the groomes at Court is dead at Salisbury; so that the King and Queen are speedily to be all gone to Wilton. So God preserve us!

13th. (Lord's day.) It being very wet all day, clearing all matters, and giving instructions in writing to my executors, thereby perfecting the whole business of my will, to my very great joy; so that I shall be in much better state of soul, I hope, if it should please the Lord to call me away this sickly time. I find myself worth, besides Brampton estates, the sum of 2,164*l*, for which the Lord be praised!

14th. To Sir G. Carteret; and, among other things, he told me, that he was not for the fanfaroone, to make a show with a great title, as he might have had long since, but the main thing, to get an estate; and another thing, speaking of minding of business – 'By G–d,' says he, 'I will, and have already almost brought it to that pass, that the King shall not be able to whip a cat, but I mean to be at the tail of it!' meaning, so necessary he is, and the King and my Lord Treasurer all do confess it, which, while I mind my business, is my own case in this office of the Navy. After dinner, beat Captain Cocke at billiards; won about 8*s* off him and my Lord Brouncker. This night I did present my wife with a diamond ring, awhile since given me by Mr Vines's brother, for helping him to be a purser, valued at about 10*l*, the first thing of that nature I did give her. Great fears we have that the plague will be a great Bill this week.

15th. It was dark before I could get home, and so land at church-yard stairs, where, to my great trouble, I met a dead corpse of the plague, in the narrow ally, just bringing down a little pair of stairs. But I thank God I was not much disturbed at it. However, I shall beware of being late abroad again.

16th. To the Exchange, where I have not been a great while. But, Lord! how sad a sight it is to see the streets empty of people, and very few upon the 'Change. Jealous of every door that one sees shut up, lest it should be the plague; and about us two shops in three, if not more, generally shut up. This day, I had the ill news from Dagenhams, that my poor Lord of Hinchingbroke his indisposition is turned to the small-pox. Poor gentleman! that he should be come from France so soon to fall sick, and of that disease too, when he should be gone to see a fine lady, his mistress! I am most heartily sorry for it.

18th. To Sheernesse, where we walked up and down, laying out the ground to be taken in for a yard to lay provisions for cleaning and repairing of ships, and a most proper place it is for the purpose. Late in the dark to Gravesend, where great is the plague, and I troubled to stay there so long for the tide.

20th. (Lord's day.) Sir G. Carteret came and walked by my bedside half an hour, talking, and telling how my Lord is unblameable in all this ill success, he having followed orders; and that all ought to be imputed to the falseness of the King of Denmark, who, he told me as a secret, had promised to deliver up the Dutch ships to us; and we expected no less; and swears it will, and will easily, be the ruin of him and his kingdom, if we fall out with him, as we must in honour do; but that all that can be, must be to get the fleet out again, to intercept De Witt, who certainly will be coming home with the East India fleet, he being gone thither. I up, and to walk forth to see the place; and I find it to be a very noble seat in a noble forest, with the noblest prospect towards Windsor, and round about over many counties, that can be desired; but otherwise a very melancholy place, and little variety, save only trees. So took horse for Staines, and thence to Branford, to Mr Povy's. Mr

Povy not being at home, I lost my labour – only ate and drank there with his lady, and told my bad news, and hear the plague is round about them there. So away to Branford; and there, at the inn that goes down to the water-side, I alight and paid off my post-horses, and so slipped on my shoes, and laid my things by, the tide not serving, and to church, where a dull sermon, and many Londoners. After church, to my inn, and eat and drank, and so about seven o'clock by water, and got, between nine and ten, to Queenhive, very dark; and I could not get my waterman to go elsewhere, for fear of the plague. Thence with a lanthorn, in great fear of meeting of dead corpses, carrying to be buried; but, blessed be God! met none, but did see now and then a link, which is the mark of them, at a distance.

21st. Called up, by message from my Lord Brouncker, and the rest of my fellows, that they will meet me at the Duke of Albemarle's this morning; so I up, and weary, however, got thither before them, and spoke with my Lord, and with him and other gentlemen to walk in the Park, where, I perceive, he spends much of his time, having no whither else to go; and here I heard him speak of some Presbyter people that he caused to be apprehended yesterday, at a private meeting in Covent Garden, which he would have released upon paying 5*l* per man for the poor, but it was answered, they would not pay anything: so he ordered them to another prison from the guard. By and by comes my fellow-officers, and the Duke walked in, and to counsel with us; and that being done, we parted, and Sir W. Batten and I to the office, where, after business, I to his house to dinner, whither comes Captain Cocke, for whose epicurism a dish of partridges was sent for. Thence to my Lord Brouncker, at Greenwich, to look after the lodgings appointed for us there for our office, which do by no means please us; they being in the heart of all the labourers and workmen there, which makes it as unsafe as to be, I think, at London. Mr Hugh May, who is a most ingenuous man, did show us the lodgings, and his acquaintance I am desirous of. Messengers went to get a boat for me, to carry me to Woolwich, but all to no purpose: so I was forced to walk it in the dark, at ten o'clock at night, with Sir J. Minnes's George with me, being mightily troubled for fear of the dogs at Coome farm, and more for fear of rogues by the way, and yet more because of the plague which is there, which is very strange, it being a single house, all alone from the town, but it seems they used to admit beggars, for their own safety, to lie in their barns, and they brought it to them. To my wife, and having first viewed her last piece of drawing since I saw her, which is seven or eight days, which pleases me beyond anything in the world, to bed, with great content, but weary.

22nd. Up, and being importuned by my wife and her two maids, which are both good wenches, for me to buy a necklace of pearl for her, and I promising to give her one of 60*l* in two years at furthest, and less if she pleases me in her painting. I went away, and walked to Greenwich, in my way seeing a coffin with a dead body therein, dead of the plague, lying in an open close belonging to Coome farm, which was carried out last night, and the parish have not appointed any body to bury it; but only set a watch there all day and night, that nobody should go thither or come thence: this disease making us more cruel to one another than we are to dogs. Walked to Redriffe, troubled to go through the little lane, where the plague is, but did, and took water and home, where all well.

25th. This day I am told that Dr Burnett, my physician, is this morning dead of the plague; which is strange, his man dying so long ago, and his house this month open again. Now himself dead. Poor unfortunate man!

26th. With Mr Andrews and Mr Yeabsly, talking about their business. We parted at my Lord Brouncker's door, where I went in, having never been there before, and there he made a noble entertainment for Sir J. Minnes, myself, and Captain Cooke, none else, saving some painted lady that dined there: I know not who she is. But very merry we were, and after dinner into the garden, and to see his and her chamber, where some good pictures, and a very handsome young woman for my Lady's woman. By water home, in my way seeing a man taken up dead, out of the hold of a small catch that lay at Deptford. I doubt it might be the plague, which, with the thought of Dr Burnett, did something disturb me. So home, sooner than ordinary, and, after supper, to read melancholy alone, and then to bed.

28th. To Mr Colvill, the goldsmith's, having not for some days been in the streets; but now how few people I see, and those looking like people that had taken leave of the world. To the Exchange, and there was not fifty people upon it, and but few more like to be, as they told me. I think to take adieu today of the London streets. In much the best posture I ever was in, in my life both as to the quantity and the certainty I have of the money I am worth; having most of it in my hand. But then this is a trouble to me what to do with it, being myself this day going to be wholly at Woolwich; but, for the present, I am resolved to venture it in an iron chest – at least, for a while. Just now comes news that the fleet is gone, or going this day, out again, for which God be praised! and my Lord Sandwich hath done himself great right in it, in getting so soon out again. I met my wife walking to the water-side, with her painter, Mr Browne, and her maids. There I met Commissioner Pett, and my Lord Brouncker, and the lady at his house had been there today, to see her.

29th. To Greenwich, and called at Sir Theophilus Biddulph's, a sober, discreet man, to discourse of the preventing of the plague in Greenwich, and Woolwich, and Deptford, where in every place it begins to grow very great.

30th. Abroad and met with Hadley, our clerk, who, upon me asking how the plague goes, told me it increases much, and much in our parish; for, says he, there died nine this week, though I have returned but six: which is a very ill practice, and makes me think it is so in other places; and therefore the plague much greater than people take it to be. I went forth, and walked towards Moorefields to see, God forgive my presumption! whether I could see any dead corpse going to the grave; but, as God would have it, did not. But Lord! how everybody's looks, and discourse in the street, is of death, and nothing else; and few people going up and down, that the town is like a place distressed and forsaken.

31st. Up: and, after putting several things in order to my removal, to Woolwich; the plague having a great increase this week, beyond all expectation, of almost 2,000, making the general Bill 7,000, odd 100; and the plague above 6,000. Thus this month ends with great sadness upon the public, through the greatness of the plague every where through the kingdom almost. Every day sadder and sadder news of its increase. In the City died this week 7,496, and of them 6,102 of the plague. But it is feared that the true number of the dead this week is near 10,000, partly from the poor that cannot be taken notice of, through the greatness of the number, and partly from the Quakers and others that will not have any bell ring for them. Our fleet gone out to find the Dutch, we having about 100 sail in our fleet, and in them the Sovereign one; so that it is a better fleet than the former with which the Duke was. All our fear is, that the Dutch should be got in before them; which would be a very great sorrow to the public, and to me particularly, for my Lord Sandwich's sake: a great deal of money being spent, and the kingdom not in a condition to spare, nor a parliament, without much difficulty to meet, to give more. And to that; to have it said, what hath been done by our late fleets? As to myself, I am very well, only in fear of the plague, and as much of an ague, by being forced to go early and late to Woolwich, and my family to lie there continually. My late greetings have been very great, to my great content, and am likely to have yet a few more profitable jobs in a little while; for which Tangier and Sir W. Warren I am wholly obliged to.

September 1665

3rd. (Lord's day.) Up, and put on my coloured silk suit very fine, and my new periwigg, bought a good while since, but durst not wear, because the plague was in Westminster when I bought it; and it is a wonder what will be the fashion after the plague is done, as to periwiggs, for nobody will dare to buy any hair, for fear of the infection, that it had been cut off the heads of people dead of the plague. I took my Lady Pen home, and her daughter Pegg; and, after dinner, I made my wife show them her pictures, which did mad Pegg Pen, who learns of the same man. My Lord Brouncker, Sir J. Minnes, and I, up to the Vestry at the desire of the Justices of the Peace, in order to the doing something for the keeping of the plague from growing; but, Lord! to consider the madness of people of the town, who will, because they are forbidden, come in crowds along with the dead corpses to see them buried; but we agreed on some orders for the prevention thereof. Among other stories, one was very passionate, methought, of a complaint brought against a man in the town, for taking a child from London, from an infected house. Alderman Hooker told us it was the child of a very able citizen in Gracious Street, a saddler, who had buried all the rest of his children of the plague, and himself and wife now being shut up in despair of escaping, did desire only to save the life of this little child; and so prevailed to have it received stark-naked into the arms of a friend, who brought it, having put it into new fresh clothes, to Greenwich; where, upon hearing the story, we did agree it should be permitted to be received and kept in the town. By water to Woolwich, in great apprehensions of an ague. Here was my Lord Brouncker's lady of pleasure, who, I perceive, goes everywhere with him; and he, I find, is obliged to carry her, and make all the courtship to her that can be.

4th. Walked home, my Lord Brouncker giving me a very neat cane to walk with; but it troubled me to pass by Coome farm, where about twenty-one people have died of the plague.

6th. To London, to pack up more things; and there I saw fires burning in the street, as it is through the whole City, by the Lord Mayor's order. Thence by water to the Duke of Albemarle's: all the way fires on each side of the Thames, and strange to see in broad daylight two or three burials upon the bankside, one at the very heels of another: doubtless, all of the plague; and yet at least forty or fifty people going along with every one of them. The Duke mighty pleasant with me; telling me that he is certainly informed that the Dutch were not come home upon the first instant, and so he hopes our fleet may meet with them.

7th. To the Tower, and there sent for the Weekly Bill, and find 8,252 dead in all, and of them 6,978 of the plague; which is a most dreadful number, and shows reasons to fear that the plague hath got that hold that it will yet continue among us. Thence to Branford, reading *The Villaine*, a pretty good play, all the way. There a coach of Mr Povy's stood ready for me, and he at his house ready to come in, and so we together merrily to Swakely, to Sir R. Viner's: a very pleasant place, bought by him of Sir James Harrington's lady. He took us up and down with great respect, and showed us all his house and grounds; and it is a place not very modern in the garden nor house, but the most uniform in all that ever I saw; and some things to excess. Pretty to see over the screen of the hall, put up by Sir J. Harrington, a long Parliament-man, the King's head, and my Lord of Essex on one side, and Fairfax on the other; and, upon the other side of the screen, the parson of the parish, and the lord of the manor and his sisters. The window-cases, door-cases, and chimneys of all the house are marble. He showed me a black boy that he had, that died of a consumption; and, being dead, he caused him to be dried in an oven, and lies there entire in a box. By and by to dinner, where his lady I find yet handsome, but hath been a very handsome woman: now is old. Hath brought him near 100,000*l*, and now he lives, no man in England in greater plenty, and commands both King and Council with his credit he gives them. After dinner, Sir Robert led us up to his long gallery, very fine, above stairs, and better, or such, furniture I never did see. A most pleasant journey we had back. Povy tells me, by a letter he showed me, that the King is not, nor hath been of late, very well, but quite out of humour;

and, as some think, in a consumption, and weary of everything. He showed me my Lord Arlington's house that he was born in, in a town called Harlington: and so carried me through a most pleasant country to Branford, and there put me into my boat, and good night. So I wrapped myself warm, and by water, got to Woolwich, about one in the morning.

10th. (Lord's day.) Walked home; being forced thereto by one of my watermen falling sick yesterday, and it was God's great mercy that I did not go by water with them yesterday, for he fell sick on Saturday night, and it is to be feared of the plague. So I sent him away to London, with his family; but another boat come to me this morning. My wife, before I come out, telling me the ill news that she hears, that her father is very ill, and then I told her I feared of the plague, for that the house is shut up. And so she much troubled, and did desire me to send them something, and I said I would, and will do so. But, before I come out, there happened news to come to me by an express from Mr Coventry, telling me the most happy news of my Lord Sandwich's meeting with part of the Dutch; his taking two of their East India ships, and six or seven others, and very good prizes: and that he is in search of the rest of the fleet, which he hopes to find upon the Wellbancke, with the loss only of the *Hector*, poor Captain Cuttle. To Greenwich, and there sending away Mr Andrews, I to Captain Cocke's, where I find my Lord Brouncker and his mistress, and Sir J. Minnes, where we supped; there was also Sir W. Doyly and Mr Evelyn; but the receipt of this news did put us all into such an ecstasy of joy, that it inspired into Sir J. Minnes and Mr Evelyn such a spirit of mirth, that in all my life I never met with so merry a two hours as our company this night was. Among other humours, Mr Evelyn's repeating of some verses made up of nothing but the various acceptations of may and can, and doing it so aptly upon occasion of something of that nature, and so fast, did make us all die almost with laughing, and did so stop the mouth of Sir J. Minnes in the middle of all his mirth, and in a thing agreeing with his own manner of genius, that I never saw any man so outdone in all my life; and Sir J. Minnes's mirth, too, to see himself outdone, was the crown of all our mirth. In this humour we sat till about ten at night, and so my Lord and his mistress home, and we to bed.

14th. To London, where I have not been now a pretty while. To the Duke of Albemarle, where I find a letter of the 12th, from Solebay, from my Lord Sandwich, of the fleet's meeting with about eighteen more of the Dutch fleet, and his taking of most of them; and the messenger says, they had taken three after the letter was wrote and sealed; which being twenty-one, and the fourteen took the other day is forty-five sail; some of which are good, and others rich ships. And, having taken a copy of my Lord's letter, I away toward the 'Change, the plague being all thereabouts. Here my news was highly welcome, and I did wonder to see the 'Change so full; I believe 200 people; but not a man or merchant of any fashion, but plain men all. And, Lord! to see how I did endeavour all I could to talk with as few as I could, there being now no observation of shutting up of houses infected, that to be sure we do converse and meet with people that have the plague upon them. I spent some thoughts upon the occurrences of this day, giving matter for as much content on one hand, and melancholy on another, as any day in all my life. For the first; the finding of my money and plate, and all safe at London, and speeding in my business this day. The hearing of this good news to such excess, after so great a despair of my Lord's doing any thing this year; adding to that, the decrease of 500 and more, which is the first decrease we have yet had in the sickness since it begun; and great hopes that the next week it will be greater. Then, on the other side, my finding that though the Bill in general is abated, yet the City, within the walls, is increased, and likely to continue so, and is close to our house there. My meeting dead corpses of the plague, carried to be buried close to me at noonday through the City in Fenchurch Street. To see a person sick of the sores carried close by me by Gracechurch in a hackney-coach. My finding the Angel Tavern, at the lower end of Tower Hill, shut up; and more than that, the Alehouse at the Tower Stairs; and more than that, that the person was then dying of the plague when I was last there, a little while ago, at night. To hear that poor Payne, my waiter, hath buried a child, and is dying himself. To hear that a labourer I sent but the other day to Dagenhams, to know how they did there, is dead of the plague; and that one of my own watermen, that carried me daily, fell sick as soon as he had landed me on Friday morning last, when I had been all night upon the water, and I believe he did get his infection that day at Branford, and is now dead of the plague. To hear that Captain Lambert and Cuttle are killed in the taking these ships; and that Mr Sydney Montagu is sick of a desperate fever at my Lady Carteret's, at Scott's

Hall. To hear that Mr Lewis hath another daughter sick. And, lastly, that both my servants, W. Hewer, and Tom Edwards, have lost their fathers, both in St Sepulchre's parish, of the plague this week, do put me into great apprehensions of melancholy, and with good reason. But I put off my thoughts of sadness as much as I can, and the rather to keep my wife in good heart, and family also.

15th. With Captain Cocke, and there drank a cup of good drink, which I am fain to allow myself during this plague time, by advice of all, and not contrary to my oath, my physician being dead, and chyrurgeon out of the way, whose advice I am obliged to take. In much pain to think what I shall do this winter time; for going every day to Woolwich I cannot, without endangering my life; and staying from my wife at Greenwich is not handsome.

16th. To the office; where I find Sir J. Minnes gone to the fleet, like a doating fool, to do no good but proclaim himself an ass; for no service he can do here, nor inform my Lord, who is come in thither to the buoy of the Nore, in anything worth his knowledge. The likelihood of the increase of the plague this week makes us a little sad. To Captain Cocke's, meaning to lie there, it being late, and he not being at home, I walked to him to my Lord Brouncker's, and there stayed a while, they being at tables: and so by and by parted, and walked to his house; and, after a mess of good broth, to bed, in great pleasure, his company being most excellent.

18th. By break of day we come to within sight of the fleet, which was a very fine thing to behold, being above 100 ships, great and small; with the flagships of each squadron, distinguished by their several flags on their main, fore, or mizen-masts. Among others, the *Soveraigne*, *Charles*, and *Prince*; in the last of which my Lord Sandwich was. And so we come on board, and we find my Lord Sandwich newly up in his night-gown very well. He received us kindly; telling us the state of the fleet, lacking provisions, having no beer at all, nor have had, most of them, these three weeks or month, and but few days' dry provisions. And, indeed, he tells us that he believes no fleet was ever set to sea in so ill condition of provision, as this was when it went out last. He did inform us in the business of Bergen, so as to let us see how the judgment of the world is not to be depended on in things they know not; it being a place just wide enough, and not so much hardly, for ships to go through to it, the yardarms sticking in the very rocks. He do not, upon his best enquiry, find reason to except against any part of the management of the business by Teddiman; he having stayed treating no longer than during the night, while he was fitting himself to fight, bringing his ship abreast, and not a quarter of an hour longer, as it is said; nor could more ships have been brought to play, as is thought. Nor could men be landed, there being 10,000 men effectively always in arms of the Danes; nor, says he, could we expect more from the Danes than he did, it being impossible to set fire on the ships but it must burn the town. But that wherein the Dane did amiss is, that he did assist them, the Dutch, all the time while he was treating with us, when he should have been neutral to us both. But, however, he did demand but the treaty of us; which is, that we should not come with more than five ships. A flag of truce is said, and confessed by my Lord, that he believes it, was hung out, but, while they did hang it out, they did shoot at us; so that it was not seen, or perhaps they would not cease upon sight of it, while they continued actually in action against us. But the main thing my Lord wonders at and condemns the Dane for is, that the blockhead, who is so much in debt to the Hollander, having now a treasure more by much than all his crown was worth, and that, which would for ever have beggared the Hollander, should not take this time to break with the Hollander, and thereby pay his debt, which must have been forgiven him, and have got the greatest treasure into his hands that ever was together in the world. By and by my Lord took me aside to discourse of his private matters, and was very free with me touching the ill condition of the fleet that it hath been in, and the good fortune that he hath had, and nothing else, that these prizes are to be imputed to. He also talked with me about Mr Coventry's dealing with him in sending Sir W. Pen away before him, which was not fair nor kind; but that he hath mastered and cajoled Sir W. Pen, that he hath been able to do nothing in the fleet, but been obedient to him; but withal tells me he is a man that is but of very mean parts, and a fellow not to be lived with, so false and base he is; which I knew well enough to be true; and did, as I had formerly done, give my Lord my knowledge of him. By and by was called a Council of War on board, when comes Sir W. Pen there, and Sir Christopher Mings, Sir Edward Spragg, Sir Joseph Jordan, Sir Thomas Teddiman, and Sir Roger Cuttance.

Great spoil, I hear, there hath been of the two East India ships, and that yet they will come into the King very rich; so that I hope this journey will be worth a 100*l* to me. So to our yacht again, having seen many of my friends there, and continued till we come into Chatham river. Among others, I hear that W. Howe will grow very rich by this late business, and grows very proud and insolent by it; but it is what I ever expected. I hear by every body how much my poor Lord Sandwich was concerned for me during my silence a while, lest I had been dead of the plague in this sickly time.

20th. Up, and after being trimmed, the first time I have been touched by a barber these twelve months, I think, and more, by and by Sir J. Minnes and Sir W. Batten met, to go into my Lord Brouncker's coach, and so we four to Lambeth, and thence to the Duke of Albemarle, to inform him what we have done as to the fleet, which is very little, and to receive his direction. But, Lord! what a sad time it is to see no boats upon the river; and grass grows all up and down White Hall court, and nobody but poor wretches in the streets! And, which is worst of all, the Duke showed us the number of the plague this week, brought in the last night from the Lord Mayor; that it is increased about 600 more than the last, which is quite contrary to our hopes and expectations, from the coldness of the late season. For the whole general number is 8,297, and of them the plague 7,165; which is more, in the whole, by above fifty, than the biggest Bill yet: which is very grievous to us all. I find Sir W. Batten and his lady gone home to Walthamstow, with some necessity, hearing that a maid-servant of theirs is taken ill.

21st. Up between five and six o'clock; and, by the time I was ready, my Lord Brouncker's coach comes for me; and taking Will Hewer with me, who is all in mourning for his father, who is lately dead of the plague, as my boy Tom's is also, I set out, and took about 100*l* with me to pay the fees at the Exchequer at Nonsuch, and so I rode in some fear of robbing. When I come thither, I find only Mr Ward, who led me to Burges's bedside, and Spicer's, who, watching of the house, as it is their turns every night, did lie long in bed today, and I find nothing at all done in my business, which vexed me. But, not seeing how to help it, I did walk up and down with Mr Ward to see the House. Walked up and down the house and park; and a fine place it hath heretofore been, and a fine prospect about the house. A great walk of an elm and a walnut set one after another in order. And all the house on the outside filled with figures of stories, and good painting of Rubens' or Holbein's doing. And one great thing is, that most of the house is covered – I mean, the posts and quarters in the walls, with lead, and gilded. I walked, also, into the ruined garden. Strange to see how young W. Bowyer looks at forty-one years; one would not take him for twenty-four or more, and is one of the greatest wonders I ever did see. I got to my Lord Brouncker's before night, and there I sat and supped with him, and his mistress, and Cocke, whose boy is yet ill. Thence, after losing a crowne betting at Tables, we walked home. Cocke seeing me to my new lodging.

27th. Up and saw and admired my wife's picture of Our Saviour, now finished, which is very pretty. By water to Greenwich, where to the King's Head, the great music

house, the first time I was ever there. Much troubled to
hear from Creed, that he was told at Salisbury, that I am
come to be a great swearer and drunkard; but, Lord! to
see how my late little drinking of wine is taken notice
of by envious men, to my disadvantage. To Captain
Cocke's, and he not yet come from town, to Mr Evelyn,
where much company; and thence in his coach with him
to the Duke of Albemarle, by Lambeth, who was in a
mighty pleasant humour; and tells us that the Dutch
do stay abroad, and our fleet must go out again, or be
ready to do so. Here we got several things ordered, as
we desired, for the relief of the prisoners, and sick and
wounded men. Here I saw this week's Bill of Mortality,
wherein, blessed be God! there is above 1,800 decrease,
being the first considerable decrease we have had. Most
excellent discourse with Mr Evelyn touching all manner
of learning, wherein I find him a very fine gentleman, and
particularly of painting, in which he tells me the beautifull
Mrs Middleton is rare, and his own wife do brave things.
Captain Cocke brought one parcel of our goods by
waggons, and I first resolved to have lodged them at
our office; but the thoughts of its being the King's house
altered our resolution, and so put them at his friend's,
Mr Glanville's, and there they are safe. Would the rest of
them were so, too! In discourse, we come to mention my
profit, and he offers me 500*l* clear, and I demand 600*l*.
We part tonight, and I lie at Mr Glanville's house, there
being none there but a maidservant and a young man,
being in some pain, partly from not knowing what to do
in this business, having a mind to be at a certainty in my
profit, and partly through his having Jacke sick still, and
his blackemore now also fallen sick. So he being gone,
I to bed.

29th. I had my horse I borrowed of Mr Gilethropp, Sir W. Batten's clerk, brought to me at Greenwich, and so set out and rode hard, and was at Nonsuch by about eight o'clock, a very fine journey, and a fine day. There I come just about chapel time, and so I went to chappel with them, and thence to the several offices about my tallies, which I find done, but strung for sums not to my purpose. But, Lord! what ado I had to persuade the dull fellows to it, especially Mr Warder, Master of the Pells, and yet without any manner of reason for their scruple. But, at last, I did, and so walked to Ewell, and to horse again, and come to Greenwich before night. Sir Martin Noell is this day dead of the plague in London, where he hath lain sick of it these eight days.

October 1665

2nd. Having sailed all night, and I do wonder how they in the dark could find the way, we got by morning to Gillingham, and thence all walked to Chatham; and there, with Commissioner Pett, viewed the Yard; and, among other things, a team of four horses come close by us, he being with me, drawing a piece of timber, that I am confident one man could easily have carried upon his back. I made the horses be taken away, and a man or two to take the timber away with their hands. To Rochester, to visit the old Castle ruins, which hath been a noble place; but, Lord! to see what a dreadful thing it is to look upon the precipices, for it did fright me mightily. The place hath been great and strong in former ages. So to walk up and down the Cathedral, and thence to the Crown, whither Mr Fowler, the Mayor of the town, was come in his gown, and is a very reverend magistrate. Took horses to Gravesend, and there staid not, but got a boat, the sickness being very much in the town still, and so called on board my Lord Brouncker and Sir John Minnes, on board one of

the East Indianmen at Erith, and there do find them full
of envious complaints for the pillaging of the ships, but
I did pacify them.

3rd. Sir W. Batten is gone this day to meet to adjourne
the Parliament to Oxford. Comes one to tell me my
Lord Rutherford is come; so I to the King's Head
to him, where I find his lady a fine young Scotch
lady, pretty handsome, and plain. My wife also, and
Mercer, by and by comes, Creed bringing them; and so
presently to dinner, and very merry. That being done,
and some music and other diversions, at last goes away
my Lord and Lady. This night, I hear that, of our two
watermen that used to carry our letters, and were well
on Saturday last, one is dead, and the other dying sick
of the plague; the plague though decreasing elsewhere,
yet being greater about the Tower and thereabouts.

5th. Among other things, talking of my sister Pall, and
my wife of herself is very willing that I should give
her 400*l* to her portion, and would have her married
soon as we could; but this great sickness time do
make it unfit to send for her up. Read a book of Mr
Evelyn's translating, and sending me as a present, about
directions for gathering a library; but the book is above
my reach, but his epistle to my Lord Chancellor is a
very fine piece. Then to Mr Evelyn's, to discourse of
our confounded business of prisoners, and sick and
wounded seamen, wherein he and we are so much put
out of order. And here he showed me his gardens, which
are, for variety of evergreens, and hedge of holly, the
finest things I ever saw in my life. Thence in his coach to
Greenwich, and there to my office, all the way having

fine discourse of trees and the nature of vegetables. Renewed my promises of observing my vows as I used to do; for I find that, since I left them off, my mind is run a wool-gathering and my business neglected.

7th. Did business, though not much, at the office, because of the horrible crowd and lamentable moan of the poor seamen, that lie starving in the streets for lack of money, which do trouble and perplex me to the heart; and more at noon, when we were to go through them, for then above a whole hundred of them followed us; some cursing, some swearing, and some praying to us. A letter come this afternoon from the Duke of Albemarle, signifying the Dutch to be in sight, with eighty sail, yesterday morning, off Solebay, coming right into the bay. God knows what they will and may do to us, we having no force abroad able to oppose them, but to be sacrificed to them. At night come two wagons from Rochester, with more goods from Captain Cocke; and in housing them come two of the Custom House, and did seize them: but I showed them my *Transire*. However, after some angry words, we locked them up, and sealed up the key, and did give it to the constable to keep till Monday, and so parted. But, Lord! to think how the poor constable come to me in the dark, going home; 'Sir,' says he, 'I have the key, and, if you would have me do any service for you, send for me betimes tomorrow morning, and I will do what you would have me.' Whether the fellow do this out of kindness or knavery, I cannot tell; but it is pretty to observe. Talking with him in the highway, come close by the bearers with a dead corpse of the plague; but, Lord! to see what custom is that I am come almost to think nothing of it.

11th. Comes up my landlady, Mrs Clerke, to make an agreement for the time to come; and I, for the having room enough, and to keep out strangers, and to have a place to retreat to for my wife, if the sickness should come to Woolwich, am to pay dear: so, for three rooms, and a dining-room, and for dinner, and bread and beer and butter, at nights and mornings, I am to give her 5*l* 10*s* per month. To Erith, and there we met Mr Seymour, one of the Commissioners for Prizes, and a Parliament-man, and he was mighty high, and had now seized our goods on their behalf; and he mighty imperiously would have all forfeited. But I could not but think it odd that a Parliament-man, in a serious discourse before such persons as we and my Lord Brouncker, and Sir John Minnes, should quote *Hudibras*, as being the book I doubt he hath read most. To Woolwich, where we had appointed to keep the night merrily; and so, by Captain Cocke's coach, had brought a very pretty child, a daughter of one Mrs Tooker's, next door to my lodgings, and so she, and a daughter and kinsman of Mrs Pett's, made up a fine company at my lodgings at Woolwich, where my wife, and Mercer, and Mrs Barbara Sheldon, danced, and mighty merry we were, but especially at Mercer's dancing a jig, which she does the best I ever did see, having the most natural way of it, and keeps time the most perfectly I ever did see. This night is kept in lieu of yesterday, for my wedding-day of ten years; for which God be praised! being now in an extreme good condition of health and estate and honour, and a way of getting more money, though at this hour under some discomfiture, rather than damage, about some prize-goods that I have bought off the fleet, in partnership with Captain Cocke, and for the discourse about the world concerning my Lord Sandwich, that he hath done a thing so bad; and indeed it must needs have been a very rash act; and the rather because of a Parliament now newly met to give money, and will have some account of what hath already been spent, besides the precedent for a General to take what prizes he pleases, and the giving a pretence to take away much more than he intended, and all will lie upon him; and not giving to all the Commanders, as well as the Flags, he displeases all them, and offends even some of the Flags, thinking others to be better served than themselves; and lastly, puts himself out of a power of begging anything again a great while of the King. Having danced my people as long as I saw fit to sit up, I to bed, and left them to do what they would. I forgot that we had W. Hewer there, and Tom, and Golding, my barber at Greenwich, for our fiddler, to whom I did give 10s.

12th. About the prize-goods, and do find that extreme ill use was made of my Lord Sandwich's order. Having learned as much as I could, which was, that the King and Duke were very severe in this point, whatever order they before had given my Lord in approbation of what he had done, and that all will come out, and the King see, by the entries at the Custom House, what all do amount to that had been taken, and so I took leave. So to Cocke, and he tells me that he hath cajolled with Seymour, who will be our friend; but that, above all, Seymour tells him that my Lord Duke did shew him today an order from Court, for having all respect paid to the Earl of Sandwich, and what goods had been delivered by his order. Good news this week that there are about 600 less dead of the plague than the last.

14th. My heart and head tonight is full of the Victualling business, being overjoyed and proud of my success in my proposal about it, it being read before the King, Duke, and the Caball with complete applause and satisfaction; this Sir G. Carteret and Sir W. Coventry both writ me. My own proper accounts are in great disorder, having been neglected about a month. This, and the fear of the sickness, and providing for my family, do fill my head very full, besides the infinite business of the office, and nobody here to look after it but myself.

16th. Up about seven o'clock; and, after drinking, and I observing Mr Povy's being mightily mortified in his eating and drinking, and coaches and horses, he desiring to sell his best, and everything else, his furniture of his house, he walked with me to Syon, and there I took water, in our way he discoursing of the wantonness of the Court, and how it minds nothing else. Upon the Exchange which is very empty, God knows! and but mean people there. The news for certain that the Dutch are come with their fleet before Margett, and some men were endeavouring to come on shore when the post come away – perhaps to steal some sheep. I walked to the Tower; but, Lord! how empty the streets are, and melancholy, so many poor, sick people in the streets full of sores; and so many sad stories overheard as I walk, everybody talking of this dead, and that man sick, and so many in this place, and so many in that.

And they tell me that, in Westminster, there is never a physician and but one apothecary left, all being dead; but that there are great hopes of a great decrease this week: God send it! At the Tower found my Lord Duke [of Albemarle] and Duchess at dinner; so I sat down; and much good cheer, the Lieutenant and his lady and several officers with the Duke. But, Lord! to hear the silly talk was there would make one mad; the Duke having none almost but fools about him. Much talk about the Dutch, in reproach of them, in whose hands the fleet is; but Lord help him! there is something will hinder him and all the world in going to sea, which is want of victuals; for we have not wherewith to answer our service; and how much better it would have been if the Duke's advice had been taken, for the fleet to have gone presently out; but God help the King! while no better counsels are given, and what is given no better taken. I have received letters from my Lord Sandwich today, speaking very high about the prize-goods, that he would have us to fear nobody, but be very confident in what we have done, and not to confess any fault or doubt of what he hath done; for the King hath allowed it, and do now confirm it, and do send orders, as he says, for nothing to be disturbed that his Lordship hath ordered therein as to the division of the goods to the fleet; which do comfort us. To the Still Yard, which place, however, is now shut up of the plague; but I was there, and we now make no bones of it. Much talk there is of the Chancellor's speech and the King's at the Parliament's meeting, which are very well liked; and that we shall certainly, by their speeches, fall out with France at this time, together with the Dutch, which will find us work.

29th. (Lord's day.) In the street, at Woolwich, did overtake and almost run upon two women crying and carrying a man's coffin between them; I suppose the husband of one of them, which, methinks, is a sad thing.

31st. Meeting yesterday the Searchers, with their rods in their hands, coming from Captain Cocke's house, I did overhear them say that his Black did not die of the plague. About nine at night I come home, and there find Mrs Pierce come, and little Frank Tooker, and Mr Hill, and other people, a great many dancing; and anon comes Mrs Coleman and her husband, and she sung very finely; though her voice is decayed as to strength, but mighty sweet though soft, and a pleasant, jolly woman, and in mighty good humour. Among other things, Laneare did, at the request of Mr Hill, bring two or three the finest prints for my wife to see that ever I did see in all my life. But, for singing, among other things, we got Mrs Coleman to sing part of the Opera, though she would not own she did get any of it without book in order to the stage; but, above all, her counterfeiting of Captain Cocke's part, in his reproaching his man with cowardice – 'Base slave,' etc. – she do it most excellently. Thus we end the month merrily; and the more that, after some fears that the plague would have increased again this week, I hear for certain that there is above 400 less; the whole number of deaths being 1,388, and of them of the plague 1,031. Want of money in the Navy puts everything out of order. Men grow mutinous; and nobody here to mind the business of the Navy but myself. I in great hopes of my place of Surveyor-General of the Victualling, which will bring me 300*l* per annum.

November 1665

4th. I hear that one of the little boys at my lodging is not well; and that they suspect, by their sending for plaister and fume, that it may be the plague; so I sent Mr Hater and W. Hewer to speak with the mother; but they returned to me, satisfied that there is no hurt nor danger, but the boy is well, and offers to be searched. After dinner, to the office, and much troubled to have 100 seamen all the afternoon there, swearing below, and cursing us, and breaking the glass windows, and swear they will pull the house down on Tuesday next. I sent word of this to Court, but nothing will help it but money and a rope.

5th. (Lord's day.) To the Cocke-pit, where I heard the Duke of Albemarle's chaplain make a simple sermon: among other things, reproaching the imperfection of humane learning, he cried 'All our physicians cannot tell what an ague is, and all our arithmetic is not able to number the days of a man' which, God knows, is not the fault of arithmetic, but that our understandings reach not the thing. I hear that the plague increases much at Lambeth, St Martin's, and Westminster, and fear it will all over the city. By water to Deptford, and there made a visit to Mr Evelyn, who, among other things, showed me most excellent painting in little; in distemper, in Indian ink, water colours; graveing; and, above all, the whole secret of mezzo-tinto, and the manner of it, which is very pretty, and good things done with it. He read to me very much also of his discourse, he hath been many years and now is about, about Gardenage; which will be a most noble and pleasant piece. He read me part of a play or two of his making, very good, but not as he conceits them, I think, to be. He showed me his 'Hortus Hyemalis'; leaves laid up in a book of several plants kept dry, which preserve colour, however, and look very finely, better than an Herball. In fine, a most excellent person he is, and must be allowed a little for a little conceitedness; but he may well be so, being a man so much above others. He read me, though with too much gusto, some little poems of his own, that were not transcendant, yet one or two very pretty epigrams; among others, of a lady looking in at a grate, and being pecked at by an eagle that was there.

7th. To Sir G. Carteret, and I with him by water: and, among other things, Lord! to see how he wondered to see the river so empty of boats nobody working at the Custom House keys, and how fearful he is: and vexed that his man, holding a wine-glass in his hand for him to drink out of, did cover his hands, it being a cold, windy, rainy morning, under the waterman's coat, though he brought the waterman from six or seven miles up the river, too. Nay, he carried his glass with him for his man to let him drink out of at the Duke of Albemarle's, where he intended to dine, though this he did to prevent sluttery: for the same reason, he carried a napkin with him to Captain Cocke's, making him believe that he should not eat with foul linnen.

8th. It being a fast-day, all people were at church, and the office quiet; so I did much business, and at noon adventured to my old lodging. By water to Deptford, and, about eight o'clock at night, did take water, being glad I was out of the town; for the plague, it seems, rages there more than ever.

9th. At noon, by water, to the King's Head at Deptford, where Captain Taylor invites Sir W. Batten and Sir John Robinson, who come in with a great deal of company from hunting, and brought in a hare alive, and a great many silly stories they tell of their sport, which pleases them mightily, and me not at all, such is the different sense of pleasure in mankind; and strange to see how a good dinner and feasting reconciles everybody. The Bill of Mortality, to all our griefs, is encreased 399 this week, and the increase generally through the whole City and suburbs, which makes us all sad.

12th. (Lord's day.) They hope here the plague will be less this week. Reading over part of Mr Stillingfleet's *Origines Sacrae*, wherein many things are very good, and some frivolous.

14th. Captain Cocke and I in his coach through Kent Street, a sad place through the plague, people sitting sick and with plaisters about them in the street begging. To the Duke of Albemarle by water, late, where I find he had remembered that I had appointed to come to him this day about money, which I excused not doing sooner; but I see, a dull fellow as he is, he do sometimes remember what another thinks he mindeth not. My business was about getting money of the East India Company; but, Lord! to see how the Duke himself magnifies himself in that he had done with the Company; and my Lord Craven what the King could have done without my Lord Duke, and a great deal of stir; but most mightily what a brave fellow I am. Back by water, it raining hard, and so to the office, and stopped my going, as I intended, to the buoy of the Nore, and great reason I had to rejoice at it, for it proved the night of as great a storm as was almost ever remembered. This day I hear that my pretty grocer's wife, Mrs Beverham, over the way there, her husband is lately dead of the plague at Bow, which I am sorry for, for fear of losing her neighbourhood.

15th. To the King's Head tavern, where all the Trinity House dined today, to choose a new Master in the room of Hurlestone, that is dead, and Captain Crispe is chosen. After dinner, who comes in but my Lady Batten, and a troop of a dozen women almost, and expected, as I found afterwards, to be made mighty much of, but nobody minded them: but the best jest was, that when they saw themselves not regarded, they would go away, and it was horrible foul weather; and my Lady Batten walking through the dirty lane with new spick and span white shoes, she dropped one of her galoshes in the dirt, where it stuck, and she forced to go home without one, at which she was horribly vexed, and I led her; and, vexing her a little more in mirth, I parted, and to Glanville's, where I knew Sir John Robinson, Sir G. Smith, and Captain Cocke were gone, and then, with the company of Mrs Pennington, whose father, I hear, was one of the Court of Justice, and died prisoner, of the stone, in the Tower, I made them, against their resolutions, to stay from hour to hour, till it was almost midnight, and a furious, dark, and rainy, and windy, stormy night, and, which was best, I, with drinking small beer, made them all drunk drinking wine, at which Sir John Robinson made great sport. But, they being gone, the lady and I very civilly sat an hour by the fireside, showing the folly of this Robinson, that makes it his work to praise himself; and all he says and do, like a heavy-headed coxcomb. The plague, blessed be God! is decreased 400; making the whole this week but 1,300 and odd; for which the Lord be praised!

20th. Up before day, and so took horse for Nonesuch, with two men with me, and the ways very bad, and the weather worse, for wind and rain. Thither, and I did get my tallies, and thence took horse, but it rained hard and blew, but got home very well. Here I find Mr Deering come to trouble me about business, which I soon dispatched, he telling me that Luellin hath been dead this fortnight, of the plague, in St Martin's Lane, which much surprised me.

22nd. I was very glad to hear that the plague is come very low; that is, the whole under 1,000, and the plague 600 and odd; and great hopes of a further decrease, because of this day's being a very exceeding hard frost, and continues freezing. This day the first of the Oxford Gazettes come out, which is very pretty, full of news, and no folly in it, wrote by Williamson. It pleased me to have it demonstrated that a Purser without professed cheating is a professed loser, twice as much as he gets.

23rd. Up betimes, and so, being trimmed, I to get papers ready against Sir H. Cholmly come to me by appointment, he being newly come over from Tangier. He did by and by come, and we settled all matters about his money, and he is a most satisfied man in me, and do declare his resolution to give me 200*l* per annum. It continuing to be a great frost, which gives us hopes for a perfect cure of the plague, he and I to walk in the park, and there discoursed with grief of the calamity of the times. I brought him home, and had a good dinner for him. Captain Cuttance tells me how W. Howe is laid by the heels, and confined to the *Royall Katherine*, and his things all seized: and how, also, for a quarrel, which indeed my Lord the other night told me, Captain Ferrers having cut all over the back of another of my Lord's servants, is parted from my Lord. We in extraordinary lack of money and everything else to go to sea next year. My Lord Sandwich is gone from the fleet yesterday towards Oxford.

24th. To London, and there, in my way, at my old oyster shop in Gracious Streete, brought two barrels off my fine woman of the shop, who is alive after all the plague, which now is the first observation or inquiry we make at London concerning everybody we know.

To the 'Change, where very busy with several people, and mightily glad to see the 'Change so full, and hopes of another abatement still the next week. I went home with Sir G. Smith to dinner, sending for one of my barrels of oysters, which were good, though come from Colchester, where the plague hath been so much. Here a very brave dinner, though no invitation; and, Lord! to see how I am treated, that come from so mean a beginning, is matter of wonder to me. But it is God's mercy to me, and his blessing upon my taking pains, and being punctual in my dealings. Visited Mr Evelyn, where most excellent discourse with him; among other things, he showed me a ledger of a Treasurer of the Navy, his great grandfather, just 100 years old; which I seemed mighty fond of, and he did present me with it, which I take as a great rarity; and he hopes to find me more, older than it. He also showed us several letters of the old Lord of Leicester's, in Queen Elizabeth's time, under the very handwriting of Queen Elizabeth, and Queen Mary, Queen of Scots; and others, very venerable names. But, Lord! how poorly, methinks, they wrote in those days, and in what plain uncut paper.

26th. (Lord's day.) Up before day to dress myself to go toward Erith, which I would do by land, it being a horrible cold frost to go by water: so borrowed two horses of Mr Howell and his friend, and with much ado set out, after my horses being frosted, which I know not what it means to this day, and my boy having lost one of my spurs and stockings, carrying them to the smith's, and I borrowed a stocking, and so got up, and Mr Tooker with me, and rode to Erith, and there on board my Lord Brouncker met with Sir W. Warren upon his business, among others, and did a great deal; Sir J. Minnes, as God would have it, not being there to hinder us with his impertinencies. To my wife at Woolwich, where I found, as I had directed, a good dinner to be made against tomorrow, and invited guests in the yard, meaning to be merry, in order to her taking leave, for she intends to come in a day or two to me for altogether. But here, they tell me, one of the houses behind them is infected, and I was fain to stand there a great while, to have their back-doors opened, but they could not, having locked them fast, against any passing through, so was forced to pass by them again, close to their sick beds, which they were removing out of the house, which troubled me: so I made them uninvite their guests, and to resolve of coming all away to me tomorrow.

28th. Up before day, and Cocke and I took a hackney-coach appointed with four horses to take us up, and so carried us over London Bridge. But there, thinking of some business, I did light at the foot of the bridge, and by help of a candle at a stall, where some pavers were at work, I wrote a letter to Mr Hater, and never knew so great an instance of the usefulness of carrying pen and ink and wax about one: so we, the way being very bad, to Nonsuch, and thence to Sir Robert Long's house – a fine place, and dinnertime ere we got thither; but we had breakfasted a little at Mr Gauden's, he being out of town though, and there borrowed Dr [Jeremy] Taylor's sermons, and is a most excellent book, and worth my buying, where had a very good dinner, and curiously dressed, and here a couple of ladies, kinswomen of his, not handsome though, but rich, that knew me by report of The. Turner, and mighty merry we were. After dinner to talk of our business, and we parted. Captain Cocke and I through Wandsworth. Drank at Sir Allen Broderick's, a great friend and comrade of Cocke's, whom he values above the world for a witty companion, and I believe he is so. So to Fox Hall, and there took boat, and down to the Old Swan, and thence to Lumbard Street – it being dark night, and thence to the Tower. Took boat, and down to Greenwich. Cocke home, and I to the office, and then to my lodgings, where my wife is come, and I am well pleased with it, only much trouble in those lodgings we have, the mistress of the house being so deadly dear in everything we have; so that we do resolve to remove home soon as we know how the plague goes this week, which we hope will be a good decrease. So to bed.

30th. At noon comes Sir Thomas Allen, and I made him dine with me, and very friendly he is, and a good man, I think, but one that professes he loves to get and to save. Great joy we have this week in the weekly Bill, it being come to 544 in all, and but 333 of the plague; so that we are encouraged to get to London soon as we can. And my father writes as great news of joy to them, that he saw York's wagon go again this week to London, and full of passengers; and tells me that my aunt Bell hath been dead of the plague these seven weeks.

December 1665

13th. Invited by Sheriff Hooker, who keeps the poorest, mean, dirty table in a dirty house that ever I did see any Sheriff of London; and a plain, ordinary, silly man I think he is, but rich – only his son, Mr Lethulier, I like, for a pretty, civil, understanding merchant; and the more by much, because he happens to be husband to our noble, fat, brave lady in our parish, that I and my wife admire so. Thence away to the Pope's Head tavern, and called to see my wife, who is well; though my great trouble is that my poor little parish is the greatest number this week in all the city within the walls, having six, from one the last week, and so by water to Greenwich. To Mr. Pierce's, where he and his wife made me drink some tea. Away to the 'Change, and there hear the ill news, to my great and all our great trouble, that the plague is increased again this week, notwithstanding there hath been a long day or two great frosts; but we hope it is only the effects of the late close, warm weather, and if the frost continue the next week, may fall again; but the town do thicken so much with people, that it is much if the plague do not grow again upon us.

22nd. I to my Lord Brouncker's, and there spent the evening by my desire in seeing his Lordship open to pieces and make up again his watch, thereby being taught what I never knew before: and it is a thing very well worth my having seen, and am mightily pleased and satisfied with it. Somewhat vexed at a snappish answer Madam Williams did give me to herself, upon my speaking a free word to her in mirth, calling her a mad jade. She answered, we were not so well acquainted yet. But I was more at a letter from my Lord Duke of Albemarle today, pressing us to continue our meetings for all Christmas, which, though everybody intended not to have done, yet I am concluded in it, who intended nothing less. The weather hath been frosty these eight or nine days, and so we hope for an abatement of the plague the next week, or else God have mercy upon us! for the plague will certainly continue the next year if it do not.

27th. Home to my wife, and angry about her desiring a maid yet, before the plague is quite over. It seems Mercer is troubled that she hath not one under her, but I will not venture my family by increasing it, before it is safe.

31st. (Lord's day.) Thus ends this year, to my great joy, in this manner. I have raised my estate from 1,300*l* in this year to 4,400*l*. I have got myself greater interest, I think, by my diligence, and my employments increased by that of Treasurer for Tangier and Surveyor of the Victualls. It is true we have gone through great melancholy because of the great plague, and I put to great charges by it, by keeping my family long at Woolwich; and myself and another part of my family, my clerks, at my charge, at Greenwich, and a maid at London; but I hope the King will give us some satisfaction for that. But now the plague is abated almost to nothing, and I intending to get to London as fast as I can. The Dutch war goes on very ill, by reason of lack of money; having none to hope for, all being put into disorder by a new Act that is made as an experiment to bring credit to the Exchequer, for goods and money to be advanced upon the credit of that Act. The great evil of this year, and the only one indeed, is the fall of my Lord Sandwich, whose mistake about the prizes hath undone him, I believe, as to interest at Court; though sent, for a little palliating it, Embassador into Spain, which he is now fitting himself for. But the Duke of Albemarle goes with the Prince to sea this next year, and my Lord is very meanly spoken of; and, indeed, his miscarriage about the prize goods is not to be excused, to suffer a company of rogues to go away with ten times as much as himself, and the blame of all to be deservedly laid upon him. My whole family hath been well all this while, and all my friends I know of, saving my aunt Bell, who is dead, and some children of my cozen Sarah's, of the plague. But many of such, as I know very well, dead; yet, to our great joy, the town fills apace, and shops begin to be open again. Pray God continue the plague's decrease! for that keeps the Court away from the place of business, and so all goes to rack as to publick matters, they at this distance not thinking of it.

January 1666

3rd. I to the Duke of Albemarle and back again: and, at the Duke's, with great joy, I received the good news of the decrease of the plague this week to seventy, and but 253 in all; which is the least Bill hath been known these twenty years in the City, though the want of people in London is it, that must make it so low, below the ordinary number for Bills. So home, and find all my good company I had bespoke, as Coleman and his wife, and Laneare, Knipp and her surly husband; and good music we had, and among other things, Mr Coleman sang my words I set, of 'Beauty, retire', and they praise it mightily. Then to dancing and supper, and mighty merry till Mr Rolt come in, whose pain of the toothache made him no company, and spoilt ours; so he away, and then my wife's teeth fell of aching, and she to bed. So forced to break up all with a good song, and so to bed.

5th. I with my Lord Brouncker and Mrs Williams by coach with four horses to London, to my Lord's house

in Covent Garden. But, Lord! what staring to see a
nobleman's coach come to town! And porters every
where bow to us; and such begging of beggars! And
delightful it is to see the town full of people again;
and shops begin to open, though in many places seven
or eight together, and more, all shut; but yet the town
is full, compared to what it used to be. I mean the
City end: for Covent Garden and Westminster are yet
very empty of people, no Court nor gentry being there.
Home, thinking to get Mrs Knipp, but could not, she
being busy with company, but sent me a pleasant letter,
writing herself, 'Barbary Allen'. Reading a discourse
about the river of Thames, the reason of its being choked
up in several places with shelves: which is plain, is by
the encroachments made upon the River, and running
out of causeways into the River, at every wood-wharf:
which was not heretofore, when Westminster Hall and
White Hall were built, and Redriffe church, which now
are sometimes overflown with water.

9th. To the office, where we met first since the plague,
which God preserve us in! Pierce tells me how great a
difference hath been between the Duke and Duchess, he
suspecting her to be naught with Mr Sydney. But some
way or other the matter is made up; but he [Sydney]
was banished the Court, and the Duke for many days
did not speak to the Duchess at all. He tells me that
my Lord Sandwich is lost there at Court, though the
King is particularly his friend. But people do speak
every where slightly of him; which is a sad story to
me, but I hope it may be better again. And that Sir G.
Carteret is neglected, and hath great enemies at work
against him. That matters must needs go bad, while

all the town, and every boy in the street, openly cries 'The King cannot go away till my Lady Castlemaine be ready to come along with him'; she being lately put to bed. And that he visits her and Mrs Stewart every morning before he eats his breakfast.

10th. I do find Sir G. Downing to be a mighty talker, more than is true, which I now know to be so, and suspected it before. To my Lord Brouncker's house in Covent Garden. The plague is increased this week from seventy to eighty-nine. We have also great fear of our Hambrough fleet, of their meeting with the Dutch; as also have certain news, that by storms Sir Jer. Smith's fleet is scattered, and three of them come without masts back to Plymouth. Seeing and saluting Mrs Stokes, my little goldsmith's wife in Paternoster Row, and there bespoke a silver chafing-dish for warming plates. To the Duke of Albemarle. Here I saw Sir W. Coventry's kind letter to him concerning my paper, and among other of his letters, which I saw all, and that is a strange thing, that whatever is writ to this Duke Albemarle, all the world may see; for this very night he did give me Mr Coventry's letter to read soon as it come to his hand, before he had read it himself, and bid me take out of it what concerned the Navy, and many things there was in it, which I should not have thought fit for him to have let anybody so suddenly see; but, among other things, find him profess himself to the Duke a friend into the inquiring further into the business of prizes, and advises that it may be publick, for the righting the King, and satisfying the people the blame to be rightly laid where it should be, which strikes very hard upon my Lord Sandwich, and troubles me to read it. Besides, the Duchess cried mightily out against the having of gentlemen captains with feathers and ribbands, and wished the King would send her husband to sea with the old plain sea Captains that he served with formerly, that would make their ships swim with blood, though they could not make leagues as Captains now-a-days can.

13th. Home with his Lordship to Mrs Williams', in Covent Garden, to dinner, the first time I ever was there, and there met Captain Cocke; and pretty merry, though not perfectly so, because of the fear that there is of a great encrease again of the plague this week. And again my Lord Brouncker do tell us, that he hath it from Sir John Baber, who is related to my Lord Craven, that my Lord Craven do look after Sir G. Carteret's place, and do reckon himself sure of it.

16th. Mightily troubled at the news of the plague's being increased, and was much the saddest news that the plague hath brought me from the beginning of it; because of the lateness of the year, and the fear we may with reason have of its continuing with us the next summer. The total being now 375, and the plague 158.

19th. It is a remarkable thing how infinitely naked all that end of the town, Covent Garden, is, at this day, of people, while the City is almost as full again of people as ever it was.

22nd. At noon my Lord Brouncker did come, but left the keys of the chest we should open, at Sir G. Carteret's lodgings, of my Lord Sandwich's, wherein Howe's supposed jewels are; so we could not according to my Lord Arlington's order, see them today; but we parted, resolving to meet here at night; my Lord Brouncker being going with Dr Wilkins, Mr Hooke, and others, to Colonel Blunt's to consider again of the business of chariots, and to try their new invention, which I saw here my Lord Brouncker ride in: where the coachman sits astride upon a pole over the horse, but do not touch the horse, which is a pretty odd thing; but it seems it is most easy for the horse, and, as they say, for the man also. The first meeting of Gresham College since the plague. Dr Goddard did fill us with talk, in defence of his and his fellow physicians going out of town in the plague-time; saying, that their particular patients were most gone out of town, and they left at liberty; and a great deal more. But what, among other fine discourse, pleased me most, was Sir G. Ent, about respiration; that it is not to this day known, or concluded on, among physicians, nor to be done either, how the action is managed by nature, or for what use is it.

23rd. Good news beyond all expectation of the decrease of the plague, being now but seventy-nine, and the whole but 272. So home with comfort to bed. A most furious storm all night and morning.

30th. Home, finding the town keeping the day solemnly, it being the day of the King's murther; and they being at church, I presently into the church. This is the first time I have been in the church since I left London for the plague, and it frighted me indeed to go through the church more than I thought it could have done, to see so many graves lie so high upon the churchyards, where people have been buried of the plague. I was much troubled at it, and do not think to go through it again a good while.

31st. I find many about the City that live near the churchyards, solicitous to have the churchyards covered with lime, and I think it is needfull, and ours, I hope, will be done. To my Lord Chancellor's new house, which he is building, only to view it, hearing so much from Mr Evelyn of it; and, indeed, it is the finest pile I ever did see in my life, and will be a glorious house. To White Hall, and, to my great joy, people begin to bustle up and down there, the King holding his resolution to be in town tomorrow, and hath good encouragement, blessed be God! to do so, the plague being decreased this week to fifty-six, and the total to 227.

February 1666

7th. It being fast-day, I staid at home all day long, putting my chamber in the same condition it was before the plague.

10th. To the office. This day comes first Sir Thomas Harvey after the plague, having been out of town all this while. He was coldly received by us, and he went away before we rose also, to make himself appear a man less necessary. To supper, and to bed, being now-a-days, for these four or five months, mightily troubled with my snoring in my sleep, and know not how to remedy it.

12th. Comes Mr Caesar, my boy's lute-master, whom I have not seen since the plague before, but he hath been in Westminster all this while, very well; and tells me, in the height of it, how bold people there were, to go in sport to one another's burials; and in spite, too, ill people would breathe in the faces, out of their windows, of well people going by.

13th. Ill news this night, that the plague is increased this week, and in many places else about the town, and at Chatham and elsewhere.

16th. To my Lord Sandwich, to talk of his affairs, and particularly of his prize goods, wherein I find he is weary of being troubled, and gives over the care of it to let it come to what it will, having the King's release for the dividend made, and for the rest he thinks himself safe from being proved to have anything more. To the Coffee House, the first time I have been there, where very full, and company, it seems, hath been there all the plague time. The Queen comes to Hampton Court tonight. With Mr Hater in the garden, talking about a husband for my sister, and reckoning up all our clerks about us, none of which he thinks fit for her and her portion.

21st. My brother John is shortly to be Master in Arts, and writes me this week a Latin letter that he is to go into orders this Lent. To the Duke's chamber, and here the Duke did bring out a book of great antiquity, of some of the customs of the Navy, about 100 years since, which he did lend us to read, and deliver him back again. To Trinity-house, being invited to an Elder Brother's feast; and there met and sat by Mr Prin, and had good discourse about the privileges of Parliament, which, he says, are few to the Commons' House, and those not examinable by them, but only by the House of Lords. Thence with my Lord Brouncker to Gresham College, the first time after the sickness that I was there, and the second time any met. And here a good lecture of Mr Hooke's about the trade of felt-making, very pretty; and anon he alone with me about the art of drawing pictures by Prince Rupert's rule and machine, and another of Dr Wren's; but he says nothing do like squares, or, which is the best in the world, like a dark room.

22nd. We are much troubled that the sickness in general, the town being so full of people, should be but three, and yet of the particular disease of the plague there should be ten increase.

March 1666

1st. Blessed be God! a good Bill this week we have; being but 237 in all, and forty-two of the plague, and of them but six in the City: though my Lord Brouncker says, that these six are most of them in new parishes, where they were not the last week.

13th. The plague increased this week twenty-nine from twenty-eight, though the totall fallen from 238 to 207.

April 1666

5th. At Viner's was shown the silver plates, made for Captain Cocke, to present to my Lord Brouncker; and I chose a dozen of the same weight to be bespoke for myself, which he told me yesterday he would give me. The plague is, to our great grief, increased nine this week, though decreased a few in the total. And this increase runs through many parishes, which makes us much fear the next year.

8th. (Lord's day.) To the Duke of York, where we all met to hear the debate between Sir Thomas Allen and Mr Wayth; the former complaining of the latter's ill usage of him at the late pay of his ship: but a very sorry poor occasion he had for it. The Duke did determine it with great judgment, chiding both, but encouraging Wayth to continue to be a check to all captains in any thing to the King's right. And, indeed, I never did see the Duke do anything more in order, nor with more judgment than he did pass the verdict in this business. The Court full this morning of the news of Tom Cheffin's death, the King's closet-keeper. He was as well last night as ever, playing at tables in the house, and not very ill this morning at six o'clock, yet dead before seven: they think, of an imposthume in his breast. But it looks fearfully among people now-a-days, the plague, as we hear, increasing every where again. To the Chapel, but could not get in to hear well. But I had the pleasure once in my life, to see an Archbishop, this was of York, in a pulpit. Then at a loss how to get home to dinner, having promised to carry Mrs Hunt thither. At last, got my Lord Hinchingbroke's coach, he staying at Court; and so took her up to Axe-yard, and home and dined; and good discourse of the old matters of the Protector and his family, she having a relation to them. The Protector lives in France: spends about 500*l* per annum. To St James's Chapel, thinking to have heard a Jesuit preach, but come too late.

9th. By coach to Mrs Pierce's, and with her and Knipp, and Mrs Pierce's boy and girl, abroad, thinking to have been merry at Chelsey; but being come almost to the house by coach near the water-side, a house alone – I think the Swan, a gentleman walking by called to us to tell us that the house was shut up of the sickness. So we, with great affright, turned back, being holden to the gentleman; and went away, I, for my part, in great disorder, for Kensington.

22nd. (Lord's day.) Up, and put on my new black coat long down to my knees. To White Hall, where all in deep mourning for the Queen's mother. To the Queen's Chapel at St James's, and there saw a little mayd baptised: many parts and words whereof are the same with that of our Liturgy, and little that is more ceremonious than ours. To Worcester House, and there stayed and saw the Council up. Back to the Cockepitt, and there took my leave of the Duke of Albemarle, who is going tomorrow to sea. He seems mightily pleased with me, which I am glad of; but I do find infinitely my concernment in being careful to appear to the King and Duke to continue my care of his business, and to be found diligent as I used to be. Sat a great while with Will Joyce, who come to see me the first time since the plague, and find him the same impertinent, prating coxcomb that ever he was.

23rd. To White Hall, where I had the opportunity to take leave of the Prince, and again of the Duke of Albemarle: and saw them kiss the King's hand and the Duke's; and much content, indeed, there seems to be in all people at their going to sea, and they promise themselves much good from them. This morning the House of Parliament do meet, only to adjourn again till winter. The plague, I hear, increases in the town much and exceedingly in the country everywhere. Bonfires in the street, for being St Georges Day, and the King's Coronation, and the day of the Prince and Duke's going to sea.

25th. I to the office, where Mr Prin come to meet about the Chest-business; and till company come, did discourse with me a good while in the garden about the laws of England, telling me the main faults in them; and, among others, their obscurity through multitude of long statutes, which he is about to abstract out of all of a sort; and, as he lives and Parliaments come, get them put into laws, and the other statutes repealed, and then it will be a short work to know the law. Having supped upon the leads, to bed. The plague, blessed be God; is decreased sixteen this week.

May 1666

12th. I find my wife troubled at my checking her last night in a coach, in her long stories out of Grand Cyrus, which she would tell, though nothing to the purpose, nor in any good manner. This she took unkindly, and I think I was to blame indeed; but she do find with reason, that, in the company of Pierce, Knipp, or other women that I love, I do not value her, or mind her as I ought. However, very good friends by and by. Met Sir G. Downing on White Hall bridge, and there walked half an hour, talking of the success of the late new Act; and, indeed, it is very much, that hath stood really in the room of 800,000*l*, now since Christmas, being itself but 1,250,000*l*. And so I do really take it to be a very considerable thing done by him; for the beginning, end, and every part of it, is to be imputed to him. This day come home again my little girle Susan, her sickness proving an ague, and she had a fit soon almost as she come home. The fleet is not yet gone from the Nore. The plague increases in many places, and is fifty-three this week with us.

June 1666

6th. By water to St James's, it being a monthly fast-day for the plague. There we all met, and did our business as usual with the Duke. By and by walking a little further, Sir Philip Frowde did meet the Duke with an express to Sir W. Coventry, who was by, from Captain Taylor, the Storekeeper at Harwich, being the narration of Captain Hayward of the *Dunkirke*; who gives a very serious account, how upon Monday the two fleets fought all day, till seven at night, and then the whole fleet of Dutch did betake themselves to a very plain flight, and never looked back again. That Sir Christopher Mings is wounded in the leg; that the General is well. That it is conceived reasonably, that of all the Dutch fleet, which, with what recruits they had, come to 100 sail, there is not above fifty got home: and of them, few, if any, of their flags. And that little Captain Bell, in one of the fire-ships, did at the end of the day fire a ship of seventy guns. We were also so overtaken with this good news, that the Duke ran with it to the King, who was gone to chapel, and there all the

Court was in a hubbub, being rejoiced over head and
ears in this good news. Away I go by coach to the New
Exchange, and there did spread this good news a little,
though I find it had broke out before. And so home to
our own church, it being the common Fast-day, and it
was just before sermon; but, Lord! how all the people
in the church stared upon me to see me whisper to Sir
John Minnes and my Lady Pen. Anon I saw people
stirring and whispering below, and by and by comes
up the sexton from my Lady Ford to tell me the news,
which I had brought, being now sent into the church by
Sir W. Batten in writing, and passed from pew to pew.
But that which pleased me as much as the news, was,
to have the fair Mrs Middleton at our church, who
indeed is a very beautiful lady. My father to Hales's,
where my father is to begin to sit today for his picture,
which I have a desire to have. At home, drawing up
my vows for the rest for the year, to Christmas; but,
Lord! to see in what a condition of happiness I am, if
I would but keep myself so; but my love of pleasure is
such, that my very soul is angry with itself for its vanity
in so doing. Home, and my father and wife not coming
in, I proceeded with my coach to take a little air as far
as Bow all alone, and there turned back; but, before I
got home, the bonfires were lighted all the town over,
and I going through Crouched Friars, seeing Mercer
at her mother's gate, stopped, and light, and into her
mother's, the first time I ever was there, and find all
my people, father and all, at a very fine supper at W.
Hewer's lodging, very neatly, and to my great pleasure.
After supper, into his chamber, which is mighty fine,
with pictures and everything else, very curious. Thence
to the gate, with all the women about me, and Mrs

Mercer's son had provided a great many serpents, and so I made the women all fire some serpents. By and by comes in our fair neighbour, Mrs Turner, and two neighbours' daughters, Mrs Tite the eldest of which, a long red-nosed silly jade; the other, a pretty black girl, and the merriest sprightly jade that ever I saw. Idled away the whole night, till twelve at night, at the bonfire in the streets. Some of the people thereabouts going about with muskets, and did give me two or three vollies of their muskets, I giving them a crown to drink; and so home. Mightily pleased with this happy day's news, and the more, because confirmed by Sir Daniel Harvy, who was in the whole fight with the Generall, and tells me that there appear but thirty-six in all of the Dutch fleet left at the end of the voyage when they run home. The joy of the City was this night exceeding great.

13th. Sir H. Cholmley tells me there are great jars between the Duke of York and the Duke of Albemarle, about the latter's turning out one or two of the commanders put in by the Duke of York. Among others, Captain du Tell, a Frenchman, put in by the Duke of York, and mightily defended by him; and is therein led by Monsieur Blancford that it seems hath the same command over the Duke of York as Sir W. Coventry hath; which raises ill blood between them. And I do, in several little things, observe that Sir W. Coventry hath of late, by the by, reflected on the Duke of Albemarle and his captains, particularly in that of old Teddiman, who did deserve to be turned out this fight, and was so; but I heard Sir W. Coventry say that the Duke of Albemarle put in one as bad as he is in his room, and one that did as little. With Baity to Hales's by coach. Here I find my father's picture begun, and so much to my content, that it joys my very heart to think that I should have his picture so well done; who, besides that he is my father, and a man that loves me, and hath ever done so, is also, at this day, one of the most careful and innocent men in the world. Invited to Sir Christopher Mings's funeral, but find them gone to church. However, I into the church, which is a fair, large church, and a great chapel, and there heard the service, and staid till they buried him, and then out; and there met with Sir W. Coventry, who was there out of great generosity, and no person of quality there but he, and went with him into his coach; and, being in it with him, there happened this extraordinary case one of the most romantic that ever I heard of in my life, and could not have believed, but that I did see it; which was this:– About a dozen able, lusty, proper men come to the coach-side with tears in their eyes, and one of them that spoke for the rest begun, and said to Sir W. Coventry, 'We are here a dozen of us, that have long known and loved, and served our dead commander, Sir Christopher Mings, and have now done the last office of laying him in the ground. We would be glad we had any other to offer after him, and in revenge of him. All we have is our lives; if you will please to get his Royal Highness to give us a fire-ship among us all, here are a dozen of us, out of all which, choose you one to be commander; and the rest of us, whoever he is, will serve him! and, if possible, do that which shall show our memory of our dead commander, and our revenge.' Sir W. Coventry was herewith much moved, as well as I, who could hardly abstain from weeping, and took their names, and so parted; telling me that he would move his Royal Highness as in a thing very extraordinary, which was done. The truth is, Sir Christopher Mings was a very stout man, and a man of great parts, and most excellent tongue among ordinary men; and, as Sir W. Coventry says, could have been the most useful man at such a pinch of time as this. He was come into great renown here at home, and more abroad, in the West Indies. He had brought his family into a way of being great; but, dying at this time, his memory and name, his father being always, and at this day, a shoemaker, and his mother a hoyman's daughter; of which he was used frequently to boast, will be quite forgot in a few months as if he had never been, nor any of his name be the better by it; he having not had time to will any estate, but is dead poor, rather than rich. So we left the church and crowd. Walked to Mrs Bagwell's, and went into her house; but I was not a little fearful of what she told me but now, which is, that her servant was dead of the plague, and that she had new-whitened the house all below stairs, but that above stairs they are not so fit for me to go up to, they being not so. So I parted thence, with a very good will, but very civilly, and away to the water-side, and sent for a pint of sack, and drank what I would, and give the waterman the rest.

July 1666

4th. Thanks be to God! the plague is, as I hear, increased but two this week; but in the country, in several places, it rages mightily, and particularly in Colchester, where it hath long been, and is believed will quite depopulate the place. With the Duke, all of us, discoursing about the places where to build ten great ships: the King and Council have resolved on none to be under third-rates; but it is impossible to do it, unless we have more money towards the doing it than yet we have in any view. But, however, the show must be made to the world. In the evening, Sir W. Pen came to me, and we walked together, and talked of the late fight. I find him very plain, that the whole conduct of the late fight was ill; that two-thirds of the commanders of the whole fleet have told him so: they all saying, that they durst not oppose it at the Council of War, for fear of being called cowards, though it was wholly against their judgement to fight that day, with the disproportion of force; and then, we not being able to use one gun of our lower tier, which was a greater disproportion than the other.

Besides, we might very well have staid in the Downs without fighting, or any where else, till the Prince could have come up to them; or, at least, till the weather was fair, that we might have the benefit of our whole force in the ships that we had. He says, three things must be remedied, or else we shall be undone by this fleet. 1. That we must fight in a line, whereas we fight promiscuously, to our utter and demonstrable ruin: the Dutch fighting otherwise; and we, whenever we beat them. 2. We must not desert ships of our own in distress, as we did, for that makes a captain desperate, and he will fling away his ship, when there are no hopes left him of succour. 3. That ships, when they are a little shattered, must not take the liberty to come in of themselves, but refit themselves the best they can, and stay out many of our ships coming in with very small disableness. He told me that our very commanders, nay, our very flag-officers, do stand in need of exercising among themselves, and discoursing the business of commanding a fleet; he telling me that even one of our flag-men in the fleet did not know which tacke lost the wind, or kept it in the last engagement. He says, it was pure dismaying and fear that made them all run upon the Galloper, not having their wits about them; and that it was a miracle they were not all lost. He much inveighs upon my discoursing of Sir John Lawson's saying heretofore, that sixty sail would do as much as one hundred; and says that he was a man of no counsel at all, but had got the confidence to say as the gallants did, and did propose to himself to make himself great by them, and saying as they did; but was no man of judgement in his business, but hath been out in the greatest points that have come before them. And then, in the business of forecastles, which he did oppose, all the world sees now the use of them for shelter of men. He did talk very rationally to me, insomuch that I took more pleasure this night in hearing him discourse, than I ever did in my life in any thing that he had said.

26th. Dined at home: Mr Hunt and his wife, who is very gallant, and newly come from Cambridge, because of the sickness, with us. With my wife and Mercer to my Lord Chancellor's new house, and there carried them up to the leads, where I find my Lord Chamberlain, Lauderdale, Sir Robert Murray, and others, and do find it the most delightful place for prospect that ever was in the world, it even abashing me; and that is all, in short, I can say of it. To the office, but no news at all from the fleet.

August 1666

6th. To my Lady Montagu's, at Westminster, and there visited my Lord Hinchingbroke, newly come from Hinchingbroke, and find him a mighty sober gentleman, to my great content. In Fenchurch Street met with Mr Battersby; says he, 'Do you see Dan Rawlinson's door shut up?' which I did, and wondered. 'Why,' says he, 'after all this sickness, and himself spending all the last year in the country, one of his men is now dead of the plague, and his wife and one of his maids sick, and himself shut up'; which troubles me mightily. So home; and there do hear also from Mrs Sarah Daniel, that Greenwich is at this time much worse than ever it was, and Deptford too: and she told us that they believed all the town would leave the town, and come to London; which is now the receptacle of all the people from all infected places. God preserve us! After dinner, in comes Mrs Knipp, and I sat and talked with her, it being the first time of her being here since her being brought to bed. I very pleasant to her; but perceive my wife hath no great pleasure in her being here. However, we talked and sang, and were very pleasant. By and by comes Mr Pierce and his wife, the first time she also hath been here since her lying-in, both having been brought to bed of boys, and both of them dead. Knipp and I sang, and then I offered to carry them home, and to take my wife with me, but she would not go: so I with them, leaving my wife in a very ill humour. However, I would not be removed from my civility to them, but sent for a coach, and went with them; and in our way, Knipp saying that she come out of doors without a dinner to us, I took them to Old Fish Street, to the very house and woman where I kept my wedding dinner, where I never was since, and there I did give them a jole of salmon, and what else was to be had. And here we talked of the ill-humour of my wife, which I did excuse as much as I could, and they seemed to admit of it, but did both confess they wondered at it; but from thence to other discourse of my Lord Brouncker. They told me how poorly my Lord carried himself the other day to his kinswoman, Mrs Howard, and was displeased because she called him uncle to a little gentlewoman that is there with him, which he will not admit of; for no relation is to be challenged from others to a lord, and did treat her thereupon very rudely and ungenteely. Knipp tells me, also, that my Lord keeps another woman besides Mrs Williams; and that, when I was there the other day, there was a great hubbub in the house, Mrs Williams being fallen sick, because my Lord was gone to his other mistress, making her wait for him till his return from the other mistress; and a great deal of do there was about it; and Mrs Williams swounded at it, at the very time when I wondered at the reason of my being received so negligently. I set them both at home – Knipp at her house, her husband being at the door; and glad she was to be found to have stayed out so long with me and Mrs Pierce, and none else. Home, and there find my wife mightily out of order, and reproaching Mrs Pierce and Knipp as wenches, and I know not what. But I did give her no words to offend her, and quietly let all pass.

7th. Comes Mr Reeve, with a twelve-foot glass. Up to the top of the house, and there we endeavoured to see the moon, and Saturn, and Jupiter, but the heavens proved cloudy, and so we lost our labour, having taken pains to get things together, in order to the managing of our new glass. I receive fresh intelligence that Deptford and Greenwich are now afresh exceedingly afflicted with the sickness more than ever.

9th. Mightily pleased with a Virgin's head that my wife is now drawing of. In the evening to Lumbard Street, about money, to enable me to pay Sir G. Carteret's 3,000*l* which he hath lodged in my hands, in behalf of his son and my Lady Jemimah, towards their portion. Mrs Rawlinson is dead of the sickness, and her maid continues mighty ill. He himself is got out of the house. I met with Mr Evelyn in the street, who tells me the sad condition at this very day at Deptford, for the plague, and more at Deale, within his precinct, as one of the Commissioners for sick and wounded seamen, that the towne is almost quite depopulated.

10th. Homeward, and hear in Fenchurch Street, that now the maid is also dead at Mr Rawlinson's; so that there are three dead in all the wife, a man-servant, and maidservant. Pleased to hear of Mrs Barbara Sheldon's good fortune, who is like to have Mr Wood's son, the mastmaker, a very rich man, and to be married speedily, she being already mighty fine upon it.

September 1666

2nd. (Lord's day.) Some of our maids sitting up late last night to get things ready against our feast today, Jane called us up about three in the morning, to tell us of a great fire they saw in the City. So I rose, and slipped on my night-gown, and went to her window; and thought it to be on the back-side of Marke-lane at the farthest; but, being unused to such fires as followed, I thought it far enough off; and so went to bed again, and to sleep. About seven rose again to dress myself, and there looked out at the window, and saw the fire not so much as it was, and further off. So to my closet to set things to rights, after yesterday's cleaning. By and by Jane comes and tells me that she hears that above 300 houses have been burned down tonight by the fire we saw, and that it is now burning down all Fish Street, by London Bridge. So I made myself ready presently, and walked to the Tower; and there got up upon one of the high places, Sir J. Robinson's little son going up with me; and there I did see the houses at that end of the bridge all on fire, and

an infinite great fire on this and the other side the end
of the bridge; which, among other people, did trouble
me for poor little Michell and our Sarah on the bridge.
So down, with my heart full of trouble, to the
Lieutenant of the Tower, who tells me that it begun
this morning in the King's baker's house in Pudding-
lane, and that it hath burned down St Magnus's church
and most part of Fish Street already. So I down to the
water-side, and there got a boat, and through bridge,
and there saw a lamentable fire. Poor Michell's house,
as far as the Old Swan, already burned that way, and
the fire running further, that, in a very little time, it got
as far as the Steel-yard, while I was there. Every body
endeavouring to remove their goods, and flinging into
the river, or bringing them into lighters that lay off ;
poor people staying in their houses as long as till the
very fire touched them, and then running into boats,
or clambering from one pair of stairs, by the waterside,
to another. And, among other things, the poor pigeons,
I perceive, were loth to leave their houses, but hovered
about the windows and balconies, till they burned
their wings, and fell down. Having staid, and in an
hour's time seen the fire rage every way; and nobody,
to my sight, endeavouring to quench it, but to remove
their goods, and leave all to the fire ; and, having seen
it get as far as the Steel-yard, and the wind mighty
high, and driving it into the City; and everything, after
so long a drought, proving combustible, even the very
stones of churches; and, among other things, the poor
steeple by which pretty Mrs — lives, and whereof my
old schoolfellow Elborough is parson, taken fire in the
very top, and there burned till it fell down; I to White
Hall, with a gentleman with me, who desired to go off

from the Tower, to see the fire, in my boat; and there up to the King's closet in the Chapel, where people come about me, and I did give them an account dismayed them all, and word was carried in to the King. So I was called for, and did tell the King and Duke of York what I saw; and that, unless his Majesty did command houses to be pulled down, nothing could stop the fire. They seemed much troubled, and the King commanded me to go to my Lord Mayor from him, and command him to spare no houses, but to pull down before the fire every way. The Duke of York bid me tell him, that if he would have any more soldiers, he shall; and so did my Lord Arlington afterwards, as a great secret. Here meeting with Captain Cocke, I in his coach, which he lent me, and Creed with me to Paul's; and there walked along Watling Street, as well as I could, every creature coming away loaden with goods to save, and, here and there, sick people carried away in beds. Extraordinary good goods carried in carts and on backs. At last met my Lord Mayor in Canning Street, like a man spent, with a handkercher about his neck. To the King's message, he cried, like a fainting woman, 'Lord! what can I do? I am spent: people will not obey me. I have been pulling down houses; but the fire overtakes us faster than we can do it.' That he needed no more soldiers; and that, for himself, he must go and refresh himself, having been up all night. So he left me, and I him, and walked home; seeing people all almost distracted, and no manner of means used to quench the fire. The houses, too, so very thick thereabouts, and full of matter for burning, as pitch and tar, in Thames Street; and warehouses of oil, and wines, and brandy, and other things. Here I saw Mr Isaac Houblon, the handsome man, prettily dressed and dirty at his door at Dowgate, receiving some of his brother's things, whose houses were on fire; and, as he says, have been removed twice already; and he doubts, as it soon proved, that they must be, in a little time, removed from his house also, which was a sad consideration. And to see the churches all filling with goods by people who themselves should have been quietly there at this time. By this time, it was about twelve o'clock; and so home, and there find my guests, who were Mr Wood and his wife Barbary Shelden, and also Mr Moone: she mighty fine, and her husband, for aught I see, a likely man. But Mr Moone's design and mine, which was to look over my closet, and please him with the sight thereof, which he hath long desired, was wholly disappointed; for we were in great trouble and disturbance at this fire, not knowing what to think of it. However, we had an extraordinary good dinner, and as merry as at this time we could be. While at dinner, Mrs Batelier come to enquire after Mr Woolfe and Stanes, who, it seems, are related to them, whose houses in Fish Street are all burned, and they in a sad condition. She would not stay in the fright. Soon as dined, I and Moone away, and walked through the City, the streets full of nothing but people; and horses and carts loaden with goods, ready to run over one another, and removing goods from one burned house to another. They now removing out of Canning Street, which received goods in the morning, into Lumbard Street, and further: and, among others, I now saw my little goldsmith Stokes, receiving some friend's goods, whose house itself was burned the day after. We parted at Paul's; he home, and I to Paul's Wharf, where I had appointed a boat to attend me, and took in Mr Carcasse and his brother, whom I met in the street, and carried them below and above bridge too. And again to see the fire, which was now got further, both below and above, and no likelihood of stopping it. Met with the King and Duke of York in their barge, and with them to Queenhithe, and there called Sir Richard Browne to them. Their order was only to pull down houses apace, and so below bridge at the water-side; but this little was or could be done, the fire coming upon them so fast. Good hopes there was of stopping it at the Three Cranes above, and at Buttulph's Wharf below bridge, if care be used; but the wind carries it into the City, so as we know not, by the water-side, what it do there. River full of lighters and boats taking in goods, and good goods swimming in the water; and only I observed that hardly one lighter or boat in three that had the goods of a house in, but there was a pair of Virginalls in it. Having seen as much as I could now, I away to White Hall by appointment, and there walked to St James's Park; and there met my wife, and Creed, and Wood, and his wife, and walked to my boat; and there upon the water again, and to the fire up and down, it still increasing, and the wind great. So near the fire as we could for smoke; and all over the Thames, with one's faces in the wind, you were almost burned with a shower of fire-drops. This is very true: so as houses were burned by these drops and flakes of fire, three or four, nay, five or six houses, one from another. When we could endure no more upon the water, we to a little alehouse on the Bankside, over against the Three Cranes, and there staid till it was dark almost, and saw the fire grow; and, as it grew darker, appeared more and more; and in corners and upon steeples, and between churches and houses, as far as we could see up the hill of the City, in a most horrid, malicious, bloody flame, not like the fine flame of an ordinary fire. Barbary and her husband away before us. We staid till, it being darkish, we saw the fire as only one entire arch of fire from this to the other side the bridge, and in a bow up the hill for an arch of above a mile long: it made me weep to see it. The churches, houses, and all on fire, and flaming at once and a horrid noise the flames made, and the cracking of houses at their ruin. So home with a sad heart, and there find every body discoursing and lamenting the fire; and poor Tom Hater come with some few of his goods saved out of his house, which was burned upon Fish Street Hill. I invited him to lie at my house, and did receive his goods; but was deceived in his lying there, the news coming every moment of the growth of the fire; so as we were forced to begin to pack up our own goods, and prepare for their removal; and did by moonshine, it being brave, dry, and moonshine and warm weather, carry much of my goods into the garden; and Mr. Hater and I did remove my money and iron chests into my cellar, as thinking that the safest place. And got my bags of gold into my office, ready to carry away, and my chief papers of accounts also there, and my tallies into a box by themselves. So great was our fear, as Sir W. Batten hath carts come out of the country to fetch away his goods this night. We did put Mr. Hater, poor man! to bed a little; but he got but very little rest, so much noise being in my house, taking down of goods.

3rd. About four o'clock in the morning, my Lady Batten sent me a cart to carry away all my money, and plate, and best things, to Sir W. Rider's, at Bednall Greene, which I did, riding myself in my night-gown, in the cart; and, Lord! to see how the streets and the highways are crowded with people running and riding, and getting of carts at any rate to fetch away things. I find Sir W. Rider tired with being called up all night, and receiving things from several friends. His house full of goods, and much of Sir W. Batten's and Sir W. Pen's. I am eased at my heart to have my treasure so well secured. Then home, and with much ado to find a way, nor any sleep all this night to me nor my poor wife. But then all this day she and I and all my people labouring to get away the rest of our things, and did get Mr Tooker to get me a lighter to take them in, and we did carry them, myself some, over Tower Hill, which was by this time full of people's goods, bringing their goods thither; and down to the lighter, which lay at the next quay, above the Tower Dock. And here was my neighbour's wife, Mrs —, with her pretty child, and some few of her things, which I did willingly give way to be saved with mine; but there was no passing with any thing through the postern, the crowd was so great. The Duke of York come this day by the office, and spoke to us, and did ride with his guard up and down the City to keep all quiet, he being now General, and having the care of all. This day, Mercer being not at home, but against her mistress's order gone to her mother's, and my wife going thither to speak with W. Hewer, beat her there, and was angry; and her mother saying that she was not a 'prentice girl, to ask leave every time she goes abroad, my wife with good reason was angry; and, when she come home, did bid her be gone again. And so she went away, which troubled me, but yet less than it would, because of the condition we are in, in fear of coming in a little time to being less able to keep one in her quality. At night, lay down a little upon a quilt of W. Hewer's in the office, all my own things being packed up or gone; and, after me, my poor wife did the like, we having fed upon the remains of yesterday's dinner, having no fire nor dishes, nor any opportunity of dressing any thing.

4th. Up by break of day, to get away the remainder of my things; which I did by a lighter at the Iron gate: and my hands so full, that it was the afternoon before we could get them all away. Sir W. Pen and I to the Tower Street, and there met the fire burning, three or four doors beyond Mr Howell's, whose goods, poor man, his trays, and dishes, shovells, etc., were flung all along Tower Street in the kennels, and people working therewith from one end to the other; the fire coming on in that narrow street, on both sides, with infinite fury. Sir W. Batten not knowing how to remove his wine, did dig a pit in the garden, and laid it in there; and I took the opportunity of laying all the papers of my office that I could not otherwise dispose of. And in the evening Sir W. Pen and I did dig another, and put our wine in it; and I my Parmesan cheese, as well as my wine and some other things. The Duke of York was at the office this day, at Sir W. Pen's; but I happened not to be within. This afternoon, sitting melancholy with Sir W. Pen in our garden, and thinking of the certain burning of this office, without extraordinary means, I did propose for the sending up of all our workmen from the Woolwich and Deptford yards, none whereof yet appeared, and to write to Sir W. Coventry to have the Duke of York's permission to pull down houses, rather than lose this office, which would much hinder the King's business. So Sir W. Pen went down this night, in order to the sending them up tomorrow morning; and I wrote to Sir W. Coventry about the business, but received no answer. This night, Mrs. Turner, who, poor woman, was removing her goods all this day, good goods, into the garden, and knows not how to dispose of them, and her husband supped with my wife and me at night, in the office, upon a shoulder of mutton from the cook's without any napkin, or any thing, in a sad manner, but were merry. Only now and then, walking into the garden, saw how horribly the sky looks, all on a fire in the night, was enough to put us out of our wits; and, indeed, it was extremely dreadful, for it looks just as if it was at us, and the whole heaven on fire. I after supper walked in the dark down to Tower Street, and there saw it all on fire, at the Trinity House on that side, and the Dolphin Tavern on this side, which was very near us; and the fire with extraordinary vehemence. Now begins the practice of blowing up of houses in Tower Street, those next the Tower, which at first did frighten people more than any thing; but it stopped the fire where it was done, it bringing down the houses to the ground in the same places they stood, and then it was easy to quench what little fire was in it, though it kindled nothing almost. W. Hewer this day went to see how his mother did, and comes late home, telling us how he hath been forced to remove her to Islington,

her house in Pye Corner being burned; so that the fire
is got so far that way, and to the Old Bailey, and was
running down to Fleet Street; and Paul's is burned, and
all Cheapside. I wrote to my father this night, but the
post-house being burned, the letter could not go.

5th. I lay down in the office again upon W. Hewer's
quilt, being mighty weary, and sore in my feet with
going till I was hardly able to stand. About two in the
morning my wife calls me up, and tells me of new cries
of fire, it being come to Barking church, which is the
bottom of our lane. I up; and finding it so, resolved
presently to take her away, and did, and took my gold,
which was about 2,350*l*, W. Hewer and Jane down by
Proundy's boat to Woolwich; but, Lord! what a sad sight
it was by moonlight, to see the whole City almost on
fire, that you might see it as plain at Woolwich, as if you
were by it. There, when I come, I find the gates shut,
but no guard kept at all; which troubled me, because
of discourses now begun, that there is a plot in it, and
that the French had done it. I got the gates open, and to
Mr Shelden's, where I locked up my gold, and charged
my wife and W. Hewer never to leave the room without
one of them in it, night or day. So back again, by the
way seeing my goods well in the lighters at Deptford,
and watched well by people. Home, and whereas I
expected to have seen our house on fire, it being now
about seven o'clock, it was not. But to the fire, and there
find greater hopes than I expected; for my confidence of
finding our office on fire was such, that I durst not ask
any body how it was with us, till I come and saw it was
not burned. But, going to the fire, I find, by the blowing
up of houses, and the great help given by the workmen

out of the King's yards, sent up by Sir W. Pen, there is a good stop given to it, as well at Marke Lane End as ours; it having only burned the dial of Barking church, and part of the porch, and was there quenched. I up to the top of Barking steeple, and there saw the saddest sight of desolation that I ever saw; every where great fires, oil-cellars, and brimstone, and other things burning. I became afraid to stay there long, and therefore down again as fast as I could, the fire being spread as far as I could see it; and to Sir W. Pen's, and there eat a piece of cold meat, having eaten nothing since Sunday, but the remains of Sunday's dinner. Here I met with Mr Young and Whistler; and, having removed all my things, and received good hopes that the fire at our end is stopped, they and I walked into the town, and find Fenchurch Street, Gracious Street, and Lumbard Street all in dust. The Exchange a sad sight, nothing standing there, of all the statues or pillars, but Sir Thomas Gresham's picture in the corner. Into Moore-fields, our feet ready to burn, walking through the town among the hot coles, and find that full of people, and poor wretches carrying their goods there, and every body keeping his goods together by themselves; and a great blessing it is to them that it is fair weather for them to keep abroad night and day; drunk there, and paid twopence for a plain penny loaf. Thence homeward, having passed through Cheapside, and Newgate market, all burned; and seen Anthony Joyce's house in fire; and took up, which I keep by me, a piece of glass of the Mercers' chapel in the street, where much more was, so melted and buckled with the heat of the fire like parchment. I also did see a poor cat taken out of a hole in a chimney, joining to the wall of the Exchange, with the hair all burnt off the body, and yet alive. So home at night, and find there good hopes of saving our office; but great endeavours of watching all night, and having men ready; and so we lodged them in the office, and had drink and bread and cheese for them. And I lay down and slept a good night about midnight: though, when I rose, I heard that there had been a great alarm of French and Dutch being risen, which proved nothing. But it is a strange thing to see how long this time did look since Sunday, having been always full of variety of actions, and little sleep, that it looked like a week or more, and I had forgot almost the day of the week.

6th. Up about five o'clock, and met Mr. Gauden at the gate of the office, I intending to go out, as I used, every now and then, today, to see how the fire is, to call our men to Bishop's-gate, where no fire had yet been near, and there is now one broke out: which did give great grounds to people, and to me too, to think that there is some kind of plot in this, on which many by this time have been taken, and it hath been dangerous for any stranger to walk in the streets, but I went with the men, and we did put it out in a little time; so that that was well again. It was pretty to see how hard the women did work in the cannells, sweeping of water; but then they would scold for drink, and be as drunk as devils. I saw good butts of sugar broke open in the street, and people give and take handfuls out, and put into beer, and drink it. And now all being pretty well, I took boat, and over to Southwarke, and took boat on the other side the bridge, and so to Westminster, thinking to shift myself, being all in dirt from top to bottom; but could not there find any place to buy a shirt or a pair of gloves, Westminster Hall being full of people's goods, those in Westminster having removed all their goods, and the Exchequer money put into vessels to carry to Nonsuch; but to the Swan, and there was trimmed: and then to White Hall, but saw nobody; and so home. A sad sight to see how the river looks: no houses nor church near it, to the Temple, where it stopped. At home, did go with Sir W. Batten, and our neighbour, Knightly, who, with one more, was the only man of any fashion left in all the neighbourhood thereabouts, they all removing their goods, and leaving their houses to the mercy of the fire; to Sir R. Ford's, and there dined in an earthen platter a fried breast of mutton; a great many of us, but very merry, and indeed as good a meal, though as ugly a one, as ever I had in my life. Thence down to Deptford, and there with great satisfaction landed all my goods at Sir G. Carteret's safe, and nothing missed I could see or hear. This being done to my great content, I home, and to Sir W. Batten's, and there, with Sir R. Ford, Mr Knightly, and one Withers, a professed lying rogue, supped well, and mighty merry, and our fears over. From them to the office, and there slept with the office full of labourers, who talked, and slept, and walked all night long there. But strange it is to see Clothworkers' Hall on fire these three days and nights in one body of flame, it being the cellar full of oil.

7th. Up by five o'clock; and, blessed be God! find all well; and by water to Pane's Wharf. Walked thence, and saw all the town burned, and a miserable sight of Paul's church, with all the roofs fallen, and the body of the quire fallen into St Fayth's; Paul's school also, Ludgate, and Fleet Street. My father's house, and the church, and a good part of the Temple the like. So to Creed's lodging, near the New Exchange, and there find him laid down upon a bed; the house all unfurnished, there being fears of the fire's coming to them. There borrowed a shirt of him, and washed. To Sir W. Coventry at St James's, who lay without curtains, having removed all his goods; as the King at White Hall, and every body had done, and was doing. He hopes we shall have no public distractions upon this fire, which is what every body fears, because of the talk of the French having a hand in it. And it is a proper time for discontents; but all men's minds are full of care to protect themselves and save their goods: the Militia is in arms every where. Our fleets, he tells me, have been in sight one of another, and most unhappily by foul weather were parted, to our great loss, as in reason they do conclude; the Dutch being come out only to make a show, and please their people; but in very bad condition as to stores, victuals, and men. They are at Boulogne, and our fleet come to St Ellen's. We have got nothing, but have lost one ship, but he knows not what. Thence to the Swan, and there drank; and so home, and find all well. My Lord Brouncker, at Sir W. Batten's, tells us the General is sent for up, to come to advise with the King about business at this juncture, and to keep all quiet; which is great honour to him, but I am sure is but a piece of dissimulation. So home, and did give orders for my house to be made clean; and then down to Woolwich, and there find all well. Dined, and Mrs Markham come to see my wife. This day our Merchants first met at Gresham College, which, by proclamation, is to be their Exchange. Strange to hear what is bid for houses